Remarkable Fun Facts and Forgotten History of Love That Changed Marriage Laws Forever

Fascinating Stories of Couples Who Defied Age, Race, and the Law to Be Together.

NICCI BROCHARD
&
DR. BEN CHUBA

Remarkable Fun Facts and Forgotten History of Love That Changed Marriage Laws Forever

Fascinating Stories of Couples Who Defied Age, Race, and the Law to Be Together.

CROSSBORDER

New York, London, Quebec

Contents

Prologue

Introduction

Love makes people do ridiculous things. Take Pocahontas and John Rolfe, who managed to accidentally create America's first celebrity wedding while everyone was busy trying not to starve in Jamestown. Or consider the Roman Emperor Justinian, who rewrote centuries of law just so he could marry an actress—because apparently, when you rule half the known world, changing the entire legal system seems easier than finding a different girlfriend.

Throughout history, couples have faced down empires, defied kings, and challenged societies armed with nothing more than stubborn hearts and questionable decision-making skills. They've started wars, ended dynasties, and occasionally created entirely new countries, all in the name of love. The results have been messy, magnificent, and often completely unintended.

This collection celebrates those beautifully chaotic moments when passion collided with politics, when romance wrestled with racism, and when two people looked at centuries of established law and said, "Hold my goblet." These are the stories of couples who didn't just break rules—they obliterated them so thoroughly that lawmakers had to invent new ones.

Meet the French teenager who married her way into three different kingdoms, the American socialite whose divorce created a constitutional crisis, and the Spanish princess whose elopement literally redrew the map of Europe. Discover how a Quaker wedding in Pennsylvania accidentally legalized interracial marriage two centuries before the civil rights movement, and learn why a Victorian-era court case about polygamy ended up defining religious freedom for generations.

Some of these couples intended to make history. Most just wanted to avoid their parents' dinner parties and marry the person who made them laugh. The universe, however, had bigger plans. Their personal rebellions became public revolutions, transforming everything from inheritance laws to immigration policies to the very definition of what constitutes a legal union.

These tales span continents and centuries, featuring star-crossed lovers who were alternatively brilliant, foolish, brave, and completely unprepared for the chaos they were about to unleash. They remind us that behind every major legal precedent lurks a very human story of two people who decided that being together was worth fighting the entire world.

Prepare yourself for stolen crowns, midnight elopements, courtroom drama, and the occasional actual revolution. Love, as you'll discover, has always been a wonderfully destabilizing force—and marriage law has never quite recovered.

Chapter 1

Love in the Time of Togas –
Ancient Affairs and Legal Oddities

Welcome to the original season of "Real Housewives of Ancient Empires," where love and marriage have always been a chaotic circus (with killer costumes). If you think modern celebrity romances are messy – with their secret weddings, public feuds, and reality TV tell-alls – wait till you get a load of these ancient power couples. In this chapter, we're dishing out the dirt on four juicy tales of love that rocked empires and rattled laws. From an emperor who literally rewrote the rulebook for his showgirl sweetheart, to Romans breaking class barriers in a rom-com rebellion, to pharaohs saying "I do" to *their own siblings* (yes, you read that right), and a teenage monarch throwing a same-sex wedding extravaganza that had old-school Romans clutching their pearls – it's clear that Cupid has been stirring up drama since antiquity. Grab your popcorn (or a goblet of wine) and settle in, because history's love life is about to spill the tea.

The Emperor and the Actress: Justinian & Theodora – A Legal Latin Love Story

Once upon a time in Byzantium, a powerful man fell in love with a woman who had a very colorful past. Think of it as the original "royal falls for commoner" fairy tale – if the commoner were a sassy burlesque dancer and the royal was an Emperor who could change laws on a whim. Our leading man is Justinian I, the 6th-century Byzantine emperor known for his legal reforms and ambition. But all his law books couldn't prepare him for Theodora, the former actress slash probable striptease artist who stole his heart. She wasn't your demure, highborn princess type; Theodora started life in the lowest tier of society, the daughter of a bear trainer and an actress. Back then, "actress" was practically code for *"nightclub entertainer"*, and she had a resume that today would read more Vegas showgirl than convent schoolgirl. By her teens, Theodora was *literally* performing risqué skits on stage (one infamous legend involves her and some very enthusiastic geese – a stunt worthy of an ancient Vegas revue). In short, she was the kind of woman respectable Roman laws said a future emperor absolutely should not marry.

But Justinian was smitten. Head-over-sandals in love. And when you're an emperor-in-training sweet on a scandalous starlet, what do you do? You change the rules of course! At the time, a long-standing law (dating back to Emperor Constantine's days) forbade men of senatorial rank from marrying actresses. *Gasp!* It was like a Byzantine version of the royal family forbidding Prince Harry to wed Meghan Markle – only in this case, Meghan is a circus performer with a fan dance routine. Justinian's own family was not thrilled either; his aunt, Empress Euphemia (a stickler for propriety), nearly had a coronary at the idea of her nephew marrying "that girl from the Hippodrome." So our lovebirds did what any determined couple would: they waited. They bided their time until the roadblocks (read: disapproving relatives and pesky laws) could be removed. Lucky for Justinian, Aunt Euphemia's opposition ended when *she…* well, ended (RIP to the royal hater). And in 524 AD, Justinian pulled the ultimate power move

– he convinced his uncle, Emperor Justin, to pass a new law that basically said: *"Former actresses can marry up, thank you very much, as long as the Emperor gives it a thumbs-up."* Cheers to loopholes in love!

With the legal green light, Justinian married Theodora swiftly and splendidly. Imagine the society gossip in Constantinople: "Stop the presses! The imperial heir just wed a woman who used to dance nearly naked with birds pecking grain off her! Scandalous and fabulous!" The wedding likely had all the bling of a blockbuster event – Justinian in imperial purple, Theodora dripping in jewels instead of stage costumes. It was the ultimate glow-up for her: from showgirl to Empress. Two years later, in 527, Justinian became Emperor and crowned Theodora as Augusta (Empress) of the Eastern Roman Empire. Talk about a promotion – yesterday's *provocative performer* was now literally the most powerful woman in the empire. If that isn't the plot of a feel-good Netflix series, I don't know what is.

And Theodora proved the naysayers wrong. She wasn't just arm candy or a pretty face from the circus; she became Justinian's most trusted adviser and an accomplished ruler in her own right. This power couple ruled side by side, sharing a brain in matters of state. When riots broke out in Constantinople (the infamous Nika Riots of 532), Justinian panicked and considered fleeing the city – a total *"let's grab the private jet and get out"* moment. But Theodora squared her shoulders, basically told him to put on his big-boy crown, and delivered one of history's greatest ultimatums. She said something along the lines of: *"Emperor, darling, if you want to run, go ahead. But I'm staying – imperial purple makes a gorgeous burial shroud."* In modern terms: *"I'd rather die in my Louis Vuitton gown than live in sweats as a nobody."* Her badass speech shamed Justinian into sticking around and quelling the rebellion. Thanks to her, the throne (and their marriage) survived the chaos. (Move over, Michelle Obama – Theodora was the ultimate ride-or-die First Lady.)

Beyond the drama, Theodora used her position to champion women's rights (talk about character development: from likely teen sex worker to imperial feminist). She passed laws to ban forced prostitution and expand women's divorce rights – perhaps remembering her own rough start in life. Not exactly what people expected from a former Hippodrome hottie, huh? It's the classic tale: bad-girl-turned-Empress uses her powers for good. Theodora eventually even got canonized as a saint in the Eastern Church – which has to be the wildest retirement plan for a onetime burlesque dancer. Justinian, for his part, never wavered in his devotion. The imperial couple remained inseparable until her death, and he reportedly mourned her deeply. In the end, *The Emperor and the Actress* proved that love not only conquers all, it can rewrite the law books. It's as if a modern president fell for a pole-dancer and then amended the Constitution to marry her – outrageous, heartwarming, and a bureaucratic nightmare all at once.

When Patrician Met Plebeian: Lex Canuleia – Cupid vs. the Class System

Switching scenes to ancient Rome, let's set the stage for a classic rom-com rebellion. The time is 445 BC – centuries before swiping right, but love still finds a way. Roman society was sharply divided into two classes: the patricians (fancy old-money senators and aristocrats, basically the yacht club set) and the plebeians (commoners, from wealthy merchants down to your local tavern keeper – the *99%* of

Rome). And in this early Republic era, a strict social taboo was backed by actual law: patricians and plebeians couldn't legally marry each other. It was the ultimate class cock-block, written into Rome's very first law code (the Twelve Tables). Think *Downton Abbey*, but if it were enforced by government decree – Lady Mary simply could not run off with the cute farmer; end of story.

Of course, Cupid gives zero figs about class distinctions. We can easily imagine some star-crossed lovers in 5th-century BC Rome: perhaps a dashing young patrician guy falling for the plebeian girl who sells figs at the market, or a plebeian soldier swooning over a patrician noblewoman he's forbidden to wed. These would-be Roman Juliets and Julii (see what I did there?) were out of luck – legally, their love was DOA. This ridiculous situation did *not* sit well with the plebeians, who already resented the patricians for hogging all the political power. By 445 BC, the tension was at a boiling point. Enter our hero: Gaius Canuleius, a tribune of the plebs with the courage to shout "This is baloney!" in Latin (probably *"Stultitia est!"*). Canuleius proposed a new law to overturn the marriage ban. It was dubbed the Lex Canuleia, basically ancient Rome's version of a Love Equality Act.

The mere suggestion of mixing high-born with low-born made the Roman Senate's patrician grandpas clutch their pearls (or whatever the male equivalent is – their senatorial togas?). The consuls – Rome's co-leaders – threw a fit trying to stop it. They argued that allowing *mixed marriages* would offend the gods, disrupt the social order, maybe cause the sky to fall. One consul, in a display of primo *snobbery*, even claimed that children of patrician-plebeian unions might anger Jupiter himself. (Apparently, he thought the King of the Gods was a hardcore elitist who would smite you for marrying outside your caste. 😕) It was peak absurdity – like a politician today saying God will send lightning if a celebrity marries a commoner. The plebeians, to their credit, did an epic collective eye-roll. The gods? Really? Roman myth is full of Jupiter chasing any woman (nymph or mortal) he fancied – *cosmic moral fabric* wasn't exactly his forte. The common folk knew B.S. when they smelled it. They rallied behind Canuleius, basically telling the establishment, "We want the right to marry *who we love*, you uptight fossils!"

What followed was part political drama, part rom-com. The plebeians threatened to stop cooperating – hinting at those famous "Conflict of the Orders" tactics where they'd walk out of the city and let the patricians fend for themselves. Nothing scares an elite more than losing their workforce and possibly their army mid-war. Cupid's cause started looking a lot more reasonable when faced with an angry mob of love-struck citizens. After much standoff, the Senate caved. The Lex Canuleia passed, repealing the ban on inter-class marriages. 🎊 *Cue the confetti and lyres!* At long last, Miss Plebeian could legally become Mrs. Patrician, and vice versa. It was as if the plot of "Pride and Prejudice" got a rewrite where Elizabeth Bennet marches into Parliament and changes the law so she can marry Mr. Darcy despite his aristocratic Aunt's objections. Score one for love!

The aftermath? Probably a slew of cross-class weddings that would have made for a killer photo spread in Ancient People Magazine. Imagine the gossipy headlines: *"Baker's Daughter Marries Senator's Son – Jupiter Doesn't Throw Thunderbolts After All!"* The upper crust likely cringed at their new in-laws ("Ugh, the plebeians are coming over for Saturnalia dinner, hide the good silver!"), but over time, society adjusted. This was a key step in blurring Rome's class lines. The children of these unions were living proof that patrician DNA and plebeian DNA could co-mingle without the world ending – who knew? By modern standards, it's like the moment in *Crazy Rich Romans* when the crazy rich family accepts the not-so-rich fiancé. Sure, there was drama, but love prevailed and everyone moved on (until the next big societal feud, anyway).

So, with the Lex Canuleia, ancient Rome had its first *"Love is Love"* victory – or rather *"Love is love, even across class"*. It's a nice reminder that long before Meghan Markle crashed the royal gates or *The Crown* gave us aristocrat-commoner showmances, regular folks in tunics fought to make marriage a matter of heart, not pedigree. Cupid 1, Class System 0.

Keeping It in the Family (Literally): Egyptian Pharaohs and Their Cringe Royal Marriages

If you thought *Rome* had weird relationship drama, allow me to introduce the ancient Egyptian Pharaohs, reigning champions of the phrase "it's complicated." These god-kings took the whole "marry within your class" idea and went toxic extreme with it – by keeping marriages *entirely within the family*. We're talking sibling weddings, folks. Brother and sister, hand-in-hand, walking down the aisle of a temple, exchanging vows with a backdrop of hieroglyphs and probably a collective "eww" from any modern onlooker. The pharaohs believed in preserving the purity of their bloodline (and their divine aura), and apparently the gene pool couldn't get *too* shallow for their tastes. It's the kind of royal family tradition that makes Game of Thrones' Lannister twins look almost *quaint*. Even the notoriously inbred European Habsburgs of later history might have said, "Guys, maybe throw a second cousin in there once in a while, diversify a bit?"

So why on earth would anyone think marrying their sibling was a good idea? For the pharaohs, part of it was religious cosplay: In Egyptian mythology, the gods Osiris and Isis were brother and sister *who were married to each other*. As living gods on earth, pharaohs figured, *"Hey, if it's good enough for the gods, it's good enough for us."* Marrying your sister wasn't gross – it was *divine*. (Never mind that most other cultures would call it a therapy-inducing scandal.) Another factor was political – keeping power "all in the family" with no risk of some outsider usurping the throne via marriage. What's the easiest way to ensure your son-in-law doesn't steal your crown? Make sure your son-in-law is also your son... because he's the same person. Mind blown or rather family tree blown – straight into a loop.

Let's dish on some specific examples, because the royal Egyptian dating pool was a who's who of your own genealogy. The Ptolemies, the Macedonian Greek dynasty that ruled Egypt in the late period, were *particularly* notorious for sibling wedlock. Case in point: the famous Cleopatra VII (yes, the one who had epic romances with Julius Caesar and Mark Antony) first had to marry both of her brothers in turn, just to satisfy tradition. As a 18-year-old queen, Cleo was ceremonially wed to kid brother Ptolemy XIII (he was about 10 – ancient politics, yikes) so they could co-rule as king and queen. That marriage went about as well as you'd expect (sibling rivalry + power struggle = war; also he sort of tried to kill her... awkward). After Ptolemy XIII conveniently died in that scuffle with Caesar's help, Cleopatra then married her other brother Ptolemy XIV, who was younger than her too. That one was basically "for show," and rumor says she had him bumped off later anyway. Clearly, Cleo preferred her lovers not related to her – she ditched little bro to hook up with Mark

Antony, choosing true love (or political alliance) over keeping it creepy. Who could blame her?

And it wasn't just the Ptolemies. The practice of sibling marriage goes way back in Egypt. The pharaoh Amenhotep I (1500s BC) married his sister Ahmose-Meritamun. Ramesses II, the great Ramses the Great (1279–1213 BC), had a *huge* harem of wives and concubines, but among them was at least one of his own daughters. Yes, you read that right – being "Daddy's girl" took on a whole new, deeply uncomfortable meaning. He married his daughter Meritamen, perhaps to elevate her status or ensure a "pure" royal lineage. (We can only imagine the Father's Day cards in that family. Actually, let's not.) And remember boy-king Tutankhamun? DNA tests in modern times suggest King Tut's parents were full-on brother and sister. No surprise, Tut had frail health and deformities – the family gene pool was more like a gene puddle. *Surprise!* Inbreeding isn't great for longevity (who knew?!). Tut died at 19, possibly one of the many genetic lottery losers in a dynasty that loved to marry its own.

The daily life in such a family must have been wild. Picture a royal Egyptian dinner party: "Queen-sister, can you pass the figs? By the way, our daughter-wife is expecting a baby who's also going to be our *grandchild…* toast to that?" It's beyond soap opera levels of tangled relationships – more like a pretzel. Modern audiences might compare it to Jerry Springer Show reveals ("I married my sister and she's having my brother's baby – and we're all Pharaohs!"). Except in this case, it was totally normalized at the time in that culture. Common Egyptians usually didn't marry siblings (they weren't *that* into copying the royals' every move), but it did happen enough during certain periods that even regular folks occasionally tied the knot with close kin. Apparently, if the god-kings do it, some of the masses will follow.

From a fashion perspective (because this chapter loves its costumes), those royal weddings were splendid on the outside: golden thrones, ornate headdresses, lots of eyeliner and linen finery. The bride and groom might be decked out like Isis and Osiris incarnate – a divine couple in the flesh. It'd all look grand… until you realize the bride and groom share the same mommy. *Cringe!* Today, any notion of this is enough to make us gag and call a therapist. But for the pharaohs, it was business as usual, all in pursuit of that "pure blood" and godly image. We can only be thankful that this particular royal tradition died out (though not soon enough – the Ptolemies kept it up right until Cleopatra's siblings-all-dead saga ended the dynasty).

In summary: The Egyptian pharaohs' marital habits are a giant cautionary tale. Do not try this at home. Marrying your sibling might keep the crown in the family, but it's more creepy than crown-worthy, and the family tree ends up looking like a wreath. It's a twist on "keeping up with the Joneses" where the Joneses *are literally your own family.* The next time someone complains about nepotism or "elite inner circles" today, remind them that at least our modern elites usually stop short of *marrying their sisters.* Progress! And if you ever feel your family is weird, just remember: at least your family reunions aren't also your wedding receptions. (Thank Ra for that.)

Two Grooms for Apollo's Blessing: Emperor Elagabalus – When Rome's Party Boy Married a Guy

Our final tale is one that might just take the wedding cake – with two grooms on top. Travel with me to Rome in the 3rd century AD, where a teen emperor named Elagabalus is about to give conservative Romans the shock of their lives. If you think modern tabloids have wild headlines, Elagabalus' love life would have broken Ancient TMZ. This kid became Emperor at 14, and puberty plus absolute power turned out to be a *very* flamboyant mix. Elagabalus (also known as Heliogabalus) was basically the Miley Cyrus of Roman emperors – he came in like a wrecking ball, blurring gender lines, flouting norms, and throwing parties that made Studio 54 look like a daycare. And, oh boy, did he love stirring up scandal, especially in the marriage department.

Let's set the scene: Rome by this time wasn't exactly a paragon of virtue – they'd seen emperors with mistresses, orgies, even one who made his horse a priest (looking at you, Caligula). But Elagabalus managed to outdo them all. He had multiple wives (five, by the ripe old age of 18, including a Vestal Virgin – which was so sacrilegious it's like a Pope marrying a nun, *publicly*). But what really had Romans spit out their wine was that Elagabalus didn't limit his love to the ladies. No, our boy swung every which way and decided that *one of his great loves – a man – deserved the full royal wedding treatment.* Yes, Emperor Elagabalus married a man. In a grand ceremony. In Rome. In the third century. Talk about being ahead of your time – this was roughly 1,700 years before anyone even conceived of legal same-sex marriage, and here's Elagabalus basically saying, "Love is love, now where's my bridal veil?"

The lucky (or unlucky?) partner in this groundbreaking marriage was named Zoticus, a chariot driver and athlete from Smyrna. Zoticus was famed for his good looks and, shall we say, *physical endowments.* Elagabalus was smitten the moment he heard about this handsome stud. He summoned Zoticus to Rome with all the pomp you'd give a foreign prince – the guy arrives to a parade of servants, gifts, and likely an awkward meet-the-Emperor moment where Elagabalus practically swooned. According to one gossip (the historian Cassius Dio, who was basically the Petronius of palace gossip), when Zoticus greeted Elagabalus as "my Lord," the teen emperor sassily replied, "Don't call me Lord – I'm a Lady." You can imagine the jaws dropping around the throne room. Elagabalus loved to dress in feminine attire, play the bride, and he fully embraced the role of the imperial drama queen.

So the emperor goes all-in and marries Zoticus in a public ceremony. Picture this: one of the most powerful men in the world, decked out in silk and gold like a high priest of the sun (Elagabalus was literally a priest of a Syrian sun god), now possibly wearing a diadem and maybe even a bridal veil, standing at the altar with his male beloved. The Romans in attendance must have been bug-eyed. They were used to *some* sexual fluidity (plenty of emperors had male lovers on the side), but a state wedding between two dudes? That was new. It was the *Talk of the Empire.* Senators grumbled, moralists wailed that Rome had fallen into depravity (again). Meanwhile, Elagabalus is just vibing, probably throwing flower petals and dancing in the streets with his wedding entourage. For him, this wasn't a scandal – it was a celebration. He even reportedly referred to another male partner, a blond charioteer named Hierocles, as his "husband" and liked to play the wife himself. Basically, Elagabalus turned the imperial palace into a full-time Pride Parade, centuries before that was a thing.

One might admire his "you do you" confidence if it weren't for, well, everything else he did. This was the same emperor who served exotic foods like flamingo brains at banquets, released lions and leopards at dinner parties for fun (guests *hoped* they were declawed… surprise, sometimes not), and allegedly prostituted himself in disguise at taverns just for kicks. He was living his best life, but he was also burning through Rome's tolerance faster than you can say "scandal." Even a society as permissive as Rome had its limits, and Elagabalus found them all. The same-sex marriage was a huge red line for many. Conservative Romans were like, *"Is nothing sacred? The Emperor is supposed to be the Father of the nation, not the blushing bride!"* The fact that he'd also upended traditional religion – promoting his own sun god, El-Gabal, over Jupiter – didn't win him any friends either. So between offending the religious establishment, the military, and just about every notion of Roman decorum, young Elagabalus's honeymoon period didn't last long (pun intended).

In the end, the party crashed brutally. At 18, after four years of non-stop *extra* behavior, Elagabalus was assassinated by his own guards, likely on the orders of his fed-up grandmother (when Grandma is plotting your murder, you know you've crossed a line). His reign was cut short, but oh boy, did he leave a legacy of love and fabulosity in the annals of history. He's remembered as possibly the first ruler to *publicly* have a same-sex wedding. That's right – while modern monarchs only recently started embracing LGBTQ+ openness, this teenager did it in AD 220. Trailblazer? In a twisted way, yes. He was the original royal who said, "screw expectations, I'll marry who I want and wear what I want." Of course, he also said "I'm a god, let's slaughter a hundred bulls" and other less adorable things, so maybe not the best role model overall. But you've got to admit, as a chapter in the history of love and marriage, the Elagabalus Affair is a jaw-dropper.

So next time someone claims same-sex marriage is a modern concept, feel free to tell them about Emperor Elagabalus and his athlete hubby, and watch their eyes pop. It's a reminder that love and identity have always found a way to thumb their nose at convention – though doing it while ruling an empire might not be the safest approach!

In conclusion, what have we learned from this whirlwind tour of ancient affairs and legal oddities? For starters, love in the time of togas was just as messy, passionate, and utterly bananas as any celebrity tabloid saga today – if not more so. History isn't just dusty dates and kings; it's one long reality show featuring lovestruck rebels and rule-breakers in fabulous outfits. We saw an emperor change the law to legitimize his fairytale romance with a scandalous performer (move over, Prince Harry – Justinian did it first, and with more lawyers involved). We watched Roman commoners fight the power so they could put a ring on their high-born baes, proving that true love can topple class barriers (take that, Caste System!). We peeked (through our fingers) at Egyptian pharaohs who married their siblings to keep their dynasty "pure," giving a whole new meaning to "keeping it in the family" (and providing excellent cautionary tales for genetic counselors everywhere). And we partied with Elagabalus, the OG royal who said "love is love, gender be damned" and threw one of history's first same-sex weddings – scandalizing even decadent Rome with his bridal gown antics.

The common thread? Love makes people do wild things. It always has. Change laws, break traditions, raise eyebrows, and occasionally dry-heave (looking at you, pharaohs). Whether it's a heartthrob emperor defying the establishment or ordinary folks pushing for their right to marry, the heart wants what it wants – and woe to anyone who stands in its way. Through it all, the costumes were indeed killer: imperial purple robes, golden diadems, sparkling togas, and let's not forget Elagabalus's avant-garde drag couture. History's lovers knew how to make a statement *and* dress for the occasion.

So, dear reader, if you ever time-travel, don't be surprised to find that the ancients were just as human (and crazy-in-love) as us. They gossiped about who's marrying whom, they laughed at uptight rules, they gasped at scandalous weddings. The more things change, the more they stay the same – only with more marble statues and fewer Instagram posts. In the grand circus of humanity, love has always been the main attraction, pulling stunts both heroic and absurd. And thank the gods (and emperors) for that, because it sure makes for one hell of a story.

Chapter 2

Crown, Cross, and Cupid –
Medieval & Church Defying Unions

They say love conquers all. In medieval Europe, love didn't just conquer – sometimes it staged a coup, sparked a scandal, or upended the powers of Church and state. Welcome, dear reader, to a tour of some truly outrageous romances that made the pious folks of the Middle Ages gasp. Think of it as a mashup of love, power, scandal, and religion – with Cupid gleefully shooting arrows where they most definitely weren't supposed to go.

We'll witness a king who literally reinvented his country's religion for lust and legacy, a pair of star-crossed intellectuals whose passion outran monastic vows (and common sense), royals who played fast and loose with the incest taboos (with a little help from the Pope), and a courtroom drama that dragged private bedroom matters into the public square. It's irreverent, it's absurd, and believe it or not, it's all true. Ready for some medieval scandal? Let's dive in.

Henry VIII's Great Escalator

King Henry VIII of England was so romantically impulsive that he created an entire new church just to upgrade his love life. He had once been a champion of Catholicism (the Pope even called him "Defender of the Faith" for slamming Martin Luther). But when the Church stood between Henry and what Henry wanted... well, that was a different story

Most people give flowers or write a sappy poem when they're trying to woo someone. Henry? He gave Anne Boleyn the Church of England. Talk about a grand gesture.

In the 1520s, Henry was desperate for a male heir. His first wife, Catherine of Aragon, had given him only a daughter (Mary), and Henry was convinced God was punishing him for marrying his brother's widow (Catherine's previous marriage). So Henry asked the Pope for an annulment—basically, "Can we pretend this 20-year marriage never happened?" The Pope, tangled in politics (Catherine's nephew was the mighty Holy Roman Emperor), dragged his feet for years. He hemmed, he hawed, perhaps hoping Henry's infatuation would blow over or Catherine might quietly retire to a convent (spoiler: neither happened). In the end, the answer from Rome was a firm "Nope."

Henry's response? Essentially, "Fine, I'll do it myself." In 1534 he had Parliament declare him the Supreme Head of the Church of England. Translation: "I'm the Pope now, thanks and goodbye." He split England from the Catholic Church in order to ditch Catherine and marry his new obsession, Anne Boleyn. It was a one-man Reformation, all for the sake of love (and a son). Imagine the shock across Europe – it was like a CEO quitting his company via Twitter and launching a rival startup because the board wouldn't approve his office romance. Petty? Perhaps. But Henry got what he wanted.

When Henry and Anne married, it was like a mic-drop moment in church history. Catherine was ousted (she spent her final years exiled from court, while her daughter Mary got demoted in the line of succession – awkward). Henry was thrilled, confidently awaiting the son of his dreams. Well, life had other plans: Anne gave birth to a daughter, the future Elizabeth I (ironic, since Elizabeth would become one of England's greatest monarchs, even without a Y chromosome). Henry grumbled but believed a boy would come next.

Alas, Anne had a few miscarriages, and Henry's eye began to wander (classic Henry). Within three years, the honeymoon was over and Henry wanted Anne gone. He accused her of all sorts of outrageous things (adultery, witchcraft – you name it) to justify getting rid of her when she didn't produce a male heir. In 1536, Anne Boleyn was beheaded. Yes, he actually executed the woman he'd changed the world to marry. Harsh? Absolutely. Tudor romance was a bloody sport.

Henry moved on immediately—marrying Jane Seymour just days later. Jane actually gave him the son he so desperately wanted (the future Edward VI), though she died shortly after childbirth. (Ever the sentimentalist, Henry later called Jane his "true wife" — perhaps because she delivered the heir and didn't live long enough to disagree with him.) He'd end up with six wives in total, hence the cheery rhyme "divorced, beheaded, died, divorced, beheaded, survived." But it was that explosive marriage to Anne Boleyn that truly defied the Church. The Pope said "You can't do that!" and Henry basically said, "Watch me."

Looking back, Henry's saga is equal parts dramatic and absurd. It was the ultimate royal midlife crisis: didn't get what he wanted from the Pope, so he started his own church. You almost have to admire the audacity. But it also shows how power bends rules—Henry had enough clout to turn his personal desire into national policy. When love (and lust) collided with authority, even centuries-old religious law was no obstacle. Henry wanted what he wanted, and not even the Pope was going to stand in his way.

The Scholar and the Nun

If Henry's tale was a royal reality show, the story of Peter Abelard and Héloïse is like a steamy indie film—passionate, intellectual, and ultimately tragic (with a touch of *"medieval spicy fanfiction"* to boot). It's a 12th-century saga of a star scholar who fell in love with his star pupil, and the fallout was jaw-dropping: secret rendezvous, a scandalous pregnancy, an enraged uncle, a violent revenge, and love letters that still sing across the ages.

Peter Abelard was a celebrity philosopher of medieval Paris—a brilliant teacher with a rock-star reputation. Héloïse was his equally brilliant student, much younger and living under the care of her uncle, Canon Fulbert. Abelard took Héloïse on as his private pupil, and sure enough, teacher and student fell madly in love. (Think of a professor running off with his star student – even today that'd be front-page gossip.) It didn't take long for "extra-curricular activities" to commence. He was supposed to be teaching her Latin; instead they were discovering the language of love (in secret, of course). Abelard even wrote love poems for Héloïse that secretly made the rounds in Paris (the medieval version of going viral). Uncle Fulbert started getting suspicious. Cue the midnight lessons and stolen kisses in candlelit corners. Eventually, Héloïse became pregnant. Abelard whisked her away to his family home in Brittany, where she gave birth to a son (whom they boldly named Astrolabe—yes, like the star-mapping instrument).

To appease Héloïse's irate uncle, Abelard agreed to marry her, but they kept the wedding secret to protect his career. Héloïse herself wasn't keen on marriage (she famously said she'd rather be Abelard's mistress than his wife, preferring love without the chain of wedlock). Still, they wed quietly. But when Uncle Fulbert blabbed about it, Héloïse publicly denied the marriage to save Abelard's reputation. That made Fulbert furious. He felt duped and dishonored.

Fulbert's revenge was brutal. One night, he sent goons to Abelard's room, and they castrated him in his sleep. (Yes, they went there. Talk about a cruel twist!) Abelard awoke to a nightmare—his masculinity literally cut away and his dignity in tatters. The scandal exploded across Paris (if medieval Twitter had existed, #HotForTeacher would have been trending, guaranteed). Abelard, humiliated and broken, retreated to a monastery as a monk. A devastated Héloïse was forced into a convent. It seemed like the end of a tragic love story.

But their love refused to die. Years later, Abelard wrote a memoir in which he recounted their affair. When Héloïse read his account, it reopened all the old feelings. She wrote to him, and thus began one of history's most extraordinary correspondences. In their letters, Héloïse poured out her heart. Despite her nun's habit, she admitted that her thoughts were still filled with the memory of their passion (at one point she basically writes, "I sing the hymns but in my heart I'm thinking of our nights together"). Abelard replied with a mixture of remorse and tenderness—torn between religious guilt and enduring love.

Reading their letters today feels like peeking into a private diary. They discuss love, longing, faith, and regret with disarming frankness. It's raw and real—more *The Notebook* than a dusty theology text. In a world where forbidden love usually ended in silence, Abelard and Héloïse kept talking to each other on parchment, baring their souls in ink. Their story didn't have a conventional happy ending—they remained in their religious lives, apart. Yet in a way it did endure: legend says they were eventually buried together, side by side (aww).

Above all, Abelard and Héloïse's saga shows that passion can bloom even in a repressive era—and not even the strictest Church doctrine could extinguish it. Their love story, with all its scandal and suffering, still captivates us today, nearly a millennium later. It's as if the two lovers are whispering to us from the past: love conquers all (even if it leaves some scars).

Kissing Cousins with Papal Blessings

Marrying your cousin was generally a big no-no in medieval canon law—unless, of course, you were royalty. Then the Church might just bend the rules (or write new ones) to accommodate your *ahem* "family chemistry."

Take Ferdinand and Isabella of Spain. They were second cousins and needed the Pope's permission to marry in 1469. The catch? The permission hadn't arrived in time. No problem: they allegedly used a forged papal dispensation to get married anyway. By the time Rome figured it out, these lovebird monarchs had united two kingdoms and were too powerful to un-marry. The Pope basically shrugged and gave them an official blessing after the fact. (When you're the "Catholic

Monarchs" and you finance Columbus's trip to the New World, the Pope tends to get flexible.)

And Ferdinand and Isabella were not unique. Europe's royal families routinely married relatives to keep dynasties intact. The Habsburgs, for example, made cousin marriage an art form – their family tree looked more like a wreath, and they ended up with the infamous "Habsburg jaw" to prove it. Yet time and again, the Church granted these special dispensations – the VIP passes of medieval matrimony – to make such unions "holy." Essentially, if a king or queen wanted to marry a cousin, the Vatican would find a way to say yes.

Even England's Henry VIII (remember him?) started off on Rome's good side: he had received a papal dispensation to marry Catherine of Aragon, who was actually his late brother's widow. (Yes, the same marriage he later wanted annulled. Oh, the irony.) Officially, the Church justified these unions as necessary for the stability of kingdoms. Unofficially, the Pope was basically saying, "Alright, fine, but just this once (wink)."

It's a prime example of power trumping principle. Church law forbade incestuous unions for ordinary folks, but throw a crown into the mix and suddenly those rules were negotiable. Need a loophole? The Pope's got a pen for that. Money, politics, and influence greased the skids. One papal decree, and voila—church-approved incest at its finest.

From a modern perspective, it's equal parts gross and absurd. (Game of Thrones has nothing on real history—at least the medieval royals got the Pope's nod first!) But this was how politics worked: bloodlines and alliances mattered more than moral consistency. The almighty Church, which preached strict marriage laws, quietly handed out hall passes to the rich and powerful. In the contest between love (or at least political marriage) and religious rules, the royals usually got their way. Why? Because as far as the medieval Church was concerned, keeping monarchs happy (and on side) was often holier than sticking to the rulebook.

'Til Impotence Do Us Part

If you think modern divorce court is awkward, you haven't heard about medieval France's impotence trials. In the late Middle Ages, a wife could actually take her husband to court for being impotent – and the court could order a literal trial by sex. Yes, you read that right.

The wife would complain that hubby couldn't "perform" in the bedroom. (Medieval folks had never heard of Viagra, so this was a big deal.) The Church (obsessed with procreation in marriage) took this seriously. First came the investigative phase: friends and servants might testify about the couple's bedroom failings (imagine the gossip!). Doctors or wise older women might examine the husband's equipment and the wife's body for evidence of virginity or past intercourse. The humiliation factor was already through the roof, and it only got worse.

If all the poking, prodding, and testimony didn't settle the matter, the judge could order the ultimate ordeal: Trial by Congress – basically, a monitored sex attempt. The couple were instructed to do the deed while court-appointed inspectors waited nearby. Sometimes they hid behind a curtain; sometimes they literally stood around the bed (holding their breath, one hopes). They were even given up to two hours to attempt the act (talk about an awkward marathon). Before and after, officials would check for any tricks (like hidden vials of animal blood to fake consummation) and even examine the sheets for, well, proof of life. Talk about pressure to perform! (It sounds like a Monty Python sketch or an episode of *Medieval Jerry Springer*, but it was deadly serious.)

Not surprisingly, the gossip from these trials spread like wildfire—everyone in town would soon know whose bedroom was a flop. The entire trying event was essentially a public spectacle. It was perhaps the world's least sexy spectator sport. If you're feeling second-hand embarrassment, you're not alone — even people back then were gawking and gossiping about these trials.

If the husband somehow succeeded under these surreal conditions, hooray – marriage saved (and you can bet he'd boast about it forever). If he failed, the marriage was annulled on the spot. The wife was free to leave (and got to reclaim her dowry), and the poor guy was publicly branded "impotent." In an age when masculinity was tied to virility, that label was devastating. Some men were so desperate to avoid it that they begged for repeat trials. (One Marquis in the 1600s went through two trials by congress – he failed both times and earned eternal infamy. Talk about a stiff penalty.)

Looking back now, the whole thing seems equal parts horrifying and darkly comic. The idea of a bunch of priests and elders effectively refereeing a couple's intimate encounter is beyond absurd. It underscores how far the medieval Church would go to enforce the "marital duty" of procreation. And it makes us pretty darn grateful that modern divorce proceedings no longer involve checking anyone's nether regions in a courtroom.

In the end, these four tales prove a few things: for Henry VIII, romance trumped the Pope; for Abelard and Héloïse, passion survived even the cruelest twist; for Ferdinand and Isabella, political love rewrote the family tree; and for those French couples, well, nothing was off-limits when the Church wanted proof of consummation. Ultimately, these stories prove that when love, lust, and power collide, not even the medieval Church could keep things neat and tidy. Kings rewrote scripture for a chance at romance, scholars and nuns defied every expectation for passion's sake, rulers slipped around holy rules to marry their kin, and prudish judges turned into bedroom voyeurs in the name of morality.

It's equal parts absurd and illuminating – basically medieval history binge-worthy enough for Netflix (except it actually happened!). Human nature hasn't changed much — people will go to extreme (and extremely weird) lengths for love and desire. The only difference now is we get to laugh (and cringe) at their exploits from a safe distance in time. Who needs modern soap operas? The Middle Ages had plenty of drama, and thank heavens we no longer have live demonstrations in court!

Chapter 3

Colonial Cupid's Rogues – Love in Chains and Puritan Predicaments

Love in colonial America wasn't all powdered wigs and polite hand-kissing. In fact, some early American love stories were so scandalous, they make modern reality TV look tame. Cupid in the colonies had to navigate slave codes, Puritan moral panics, broomstick weddings, and even the occasional "back from the dead" spouse. The result? A series of romantic escapades equal parts heartwarming, heart-wrenching, and hilarious. So settle in as we journey through four unbelievable (but true!) tales of love, power, scandal, and religion from early America – with a wink and a nod to our own modern antics along the way.

From Bondage to Betrothal

Picture Maryland in 1681: a teenage Irish indentured servant – let's call her Nell – falls head over heels for an enslaved African man named (fittingly) Charles. It's the classic story of girl meets boy, girl swoons, colony loses its mind. Nell was essentially an imported laborer working off her passage to the New World. Charles was considered property under the law. By the strict social rules of the day, these two were *never* supposed to flirt, let alone plan a future together. But love, ever the troublemaker, thumbed its nose at 17th-century racial taboos. Nell and Charles announced they wanted to marry.

Now, colonial Maryland had a real doozy of a law on the books dating back to 1664. In essence, it said: *"Hey free women, if you marry an enslaved man, congrats – you just enslaved yourself for life!"* Seriously. According to the law, any free or indentured woman who dared to wed a Black slave would herself become a slave for the duration of her husband's life. And their children? Also enslaved from birth. Talk about the worst wedding gift ever – "I now pronounce you man and wife; you may kiss your freedom goodbye." This law was the big, ugly hammer designed to prevent interracial unions and keep everyone in their "proper" social box.

So when 16-year-old Nell (an indentured servant, technically still not free) said "I do" to Charles, the colonial powers-that-be flipped out. The governor of Maryland at the time, Lord Baltimore, practically spat out his tea in shock. A white Irish girl marrying an African slave? In 1681, that was the equivalent of a scandalous celebrity elopement – think a royal princess running off with someone her family absolutely forbids, but multiply the outrage by ten. Lord Baltimore was so disturbed by the idea of a white woman voluntarily entering slavery that he rushed to change the law. He petitioned the colonial assembly to repeal the whole darn thing, likely thinking, *"We can't actually let this happen; it's bad PR for our enlightened colony (and plus, ew, interracial marriage – they just couldn't handle it)."*

And the assembly did act – kind of. In 1681 they tweaked the law: instead of automatically enslaving the woman, they outright banned any marriages between indentured servants and slaves going forward. Plus, they threatened hefty fines for any slaveholder who allowed his slave to marry a white woman. Basically, "Don't even *think* about it, or it'll cost you." Sounds like progress? Eh, only in the sense of "let's prevent these marriages entirely" rather than punishing the women after the fact. A very "thanks but no thanks" attempt at reform.

But here's the kicker: Nell and Charles were too quick – or perhaps too in love – to wait. They tied the knot *before* the new 1681 ban officially took effect, seizing a brief window when the old law was still technically in play. Imagine the scene: Nell, determined and defiant, marches up to the altar (or whatever counted as an altar on a Maryland plantation) with Charles, while her employer/master is sputtering "No, no, no!" in the background like a colonial version of a Hollywood rom-com father objecting at the wedding. In that moment, Cupid's arrow beat the rulebook.

And thus, by the insane logic of the old law, Nell effectively chained herself to Charles's fate. She became the legal property of Charles's master, one Mr. William Boarman. One can only speculate how Thanksgiving dinner went that year on the Boarman estate: "Please pass the potatoes – and oh by the way, I'm now both your servant *and* your daughter-in-law. How's that for awkward?" Nell had been an indentured servant bound for a few years of work; now she was a slave, likely for life, because true love apparently demanded the ultimate sacrifice in colonial Maryland – freedom itself.

You might think this story would end with tragedy or a quick reversal – perhaps a daring escape or some deus ex machina freeing the lovers. Nope. Nell and Charles actually stayed together as a couple, living out their days enslaved on that Maryland plantation. They had seven or eight children in the years that followed. Sadly, because their marriage happened under the old racist law (even though it was repealed, it wasn't retroactive), all of their kids were born into slavery too. Love had bound Nell and Charles together, but the law made sure those bonds were literal shackles for their progeny. *Talk about a family heirloom nobody wanted.*

It gets even more dramatic: fast forward nearly 90 years. Their grandchildren and great-grandchildren are still enslaved (yeah, colonial injustice has a long half-life). Two of their descendants, a brother and sister named William and Mary Butler, decided around 1770 to sue for their freedom. Their argument? Great-Grandma Nell was a white woman, so we shouldn't be slaves! Surely even a colonial court could see the logic that white = free, right? Alas, racism's grip was tight: the Maryland judges basically said, "Nah, we can't just free people because then society would collapse – think of the chaos if we admit white lineage means freedom, so many *people* would get ideas…" In other words, they doubled down: *rules are rules, even if your ancestor was essentially tricked into slavery by Cupid.* William and Mary Butler lost their case; the court fretted that freeing them would set a too "disruptive" precedent. Heaven forbid justice disturb the status quo.

It wasn't until 1787 – over a century after Nell and Charles's fateful "I do" – that one of their descendants finally caught a break in court and was freed. And even that was on a technicality. The judges conveniently ruled that since nobody had a record of an *actual marriage certificate* for Nell and Charles (who had time to file paperwork while breaking every taboo in the book?), the old slavery-for-interracial-marriage law shouldn't have applied in the first place. Therefore, by a legal sleight of hand, Nell should never have been made a slave and so her great-granddaughter could go free. Of course, this ruling was careful not to actually challenge the racist status quo beyond that one case – the court wasn't exactly becoming an early civil rights champion. They just wanted to avoid saying "a white woman's kids can be slaves" without unleashing a freedom frenzy for others.

So what's the takeaway of Nell and Charles's saga? On one hand, it's a heartwarming tale of love conquering all – even colonial bigotry and bondage – as they chose each other against all odds. On the other hand, it's a cautionary tale that highlights the cruel absurdity of racism enshrined in law. The idea that marrying someone could change your status from servant to slave sounds like some dystopian fantasy, but it was all too real. Love, power, and scandal intertwined: their union threatened the very foundations of the slave society, so the powers in charge did everything to snuff it out or punish it. Yet, there they were, Nell and Charles, two rebels in love, quietly thumbing their noses at the establishment simply by staying together.

In modern terms, it's as if a strict high school forbade the prom queen from dating the kid from the wrong side of the tracks – and when she elopes with him, they expel her *and* ban prom for everyone forever. Harsh! You have to admire Nell's moxie: at 16, she basically told the colony "My life, my choice." It's a reminder that even in history's darkest chapters, people fell in love across color lines and social barriers, and some were brave (or crazy) enough to act on it. The colonial establishment could shackle their bodies, but not their hearts – and that defiance echoes as a twisted, inspiring love story through the ages.

Puritan Passion (and Punishment)

Now, let's leave Maryland's steamy scandal behind and head north to Puritan New England, where romance had its own special set of handicaps. If you thought *your* town was strict about public displays of affection, the Puritans would like a word. In 17th-century New England, a simple kiss could be downright criminal – literally. The Puritans didn't just frown on PDA; they criminalized it with the enthusiasm of a vice squad.

Puritans believed in keeping society on the straight and narrow (mostly straight, totally narrow). Courting – their term for dating – was serious business, with more rules than a church picnic. Young people could socialize under carefully controlled conditions, often with a chaperone within earshot or even a wooden "courting stick" to chat from a safe distance. (Yes, a hollow stick so two lovers could whisper sweet nothings from 8 feet apart. Think of it as the original "socially-distanced dating" – long before Zoom calls, they had loooong sticks). The goal was clear: no touching, certainly no canoodling, until the wedding band was firmly on the finger. Even then, keep it discreet, folks.

But of course, youth and passion being what they are, rules exist to be bent or broken. Enter one of my favorite Puritan-era scandals: the case of a kiss that caused chaos. In New Haven Colony (Connecticut) around 1660, a young woman named Sarah and a fellow named Jacob were engaged in some innocent flirtation. Picture them sitting in the parlor of a neighbor's house after a quilting bee or something. Jacob, feeling frisky (by Puritan standards), playfully snatches Sarah's glove – perhaps the 17th-century equivalent of stealing a girl's hat or teasing her on Instagram. Sarah, laughing, tries to get her glove back. Jacob grins and says something like, "I'll give it back for a kiss." Cheeky, right?

To our surprise (and probably *their* surprise in retrospect), Sarah agreed. One little kiss, okay – but these two apparently had been really, really repressed by all that strict upbringing. That "little" kiss turned into a full-on make-out session lasting half an hour. (Half an hour! In a world without Tic Tacs or toothpaste as we know it – brave souls, those two.) They must have been so absorbed in each other that they forgot the number one rule of Puritan society: *there's always a nosy witness lurking.* Sure enough, some killjoy – perhaps the very neighbor whose house it was, or some passerby with Puritan Spidey-sense tingling – caught a glimpse of the unholy lip-lock and just about dropped dead from shock.

This witness did what any good Puritan snitch would do: reported the young couple to the authorities for "sinful dalliance." Next thing Sarah and Jacob know, they're dragged into court to answer for their heinous crime of passionate necking. Can you imagine the court transcript? "The defendants did sit closelie upon a chest, his arm about her waist and her arm upon his shoulder, and did... *kiss* in a lascivious manner." I bet the magistrates read the charges with the same tone one might announce a grand larceny today. Scandalous!

In court, Sarah and Jacob got a stern talking-to about how they'd basically invited the wrath of God and undermined the moral fiber of the community by swapping spit out of wedlock. Puritan justice was swift and stern. In this case, they fined Sarah – yes, the woman, of course – for her part in the make-out misconduct, and likely gave Jacob a finger-wagging as well. Sarah paying the fine might reflect a common Puritan sentiment that women should be the guardians of virtue (Eve's daughters leading poor Adam's sons astray, yada yada). If there was any public punishment like time in the stocks, the records don't shout about it, but the shame of being officially labeled a lip-sinner in front of all your neighbors was probably punishment enough.

Lest you think this was a one-off, the Puritans had *plenty* of other ways to make budding lovers think twice. In Massachusetts, Capt. Thomas Kemble found this out the hard way in 1653. After a three-year business trip at sea (imagine three years away from your spouse – no FaceTime, not even snail mail reliably), Capt. Kemble finally returned home to Boston. Overjoyed, he walked in his front door and gave his wife a big, loving kiss. Aww, happy reunion! Except – oops – it was Sunday. And in Puritan land, you're not supposed to do *anything* on the Sabbath that isn't praying, reading scripture, or sitting dourly in church. Kissing your wife after three years? That counted as "lewd and unseemly behavior" on the Lord's Day. I kid you not. The poor man was promptly sentenced to spend two hours in the public stocks on the next market day, essentially for the crime of enthusiastic PDA under wrong timing.

Now, being put in the stocks was no picnic: you'd sit on a wooden platform in the town center with your ankles and/or wrists locked in place by boards, on display like a zoo animal, while townsfolk gawked. If they really disapproved of you, you might get a few rotten vegetables hurled your way for good measure. I can only imagine Capt. Kemble sitting there, thinking, "All this because I missed my wife and gave her a peck?!" Maybe some sympathetic neighbors whispered, "Next time, save it for Monday, Tom." The absurdity is through the roof by our standards – today he'd be trending on Twitter as #StockedForASmooch with people taking selfies next to him.

Puritan New England enforced a whole catalog of behaviors to keep everyone virtuous (or at least appearing virtuous). A quick rundown of Things That Could Get You Punished in Puritan Town:

- Kissing (or even heavy flirting) in public: Fine, public shaming, and the everlasting suspicion of the church elders. Puritan parents probably used Sarah and Jacob's tale as a cautionary bedtime story: "If you kiss before you're married, the court will know!".

- Missing Sunday church service: You'd be looking at time in the stocks. Sleep in on Sunday and you'll make up that nap with a very uncomfortable one in public.

- Celebrating Christmas: Believe it or not, the Puritans banned Christmas for a while – too pagan and rowdy! If you dared to deck the halls or (heaven forbid) take the day off to celebrate, you could be fined 5 shillings. *We see you hiding that fruitcake, John Proctor. Pay up!*

- Adultery: Now this was super serious – officially it was punishable by death in Massachusetts for a time, though executions were rare. More commonly, you'd get humiliated: whipped, forced to wear a big red "A" (sound familiar? Hello, *Scarlet Letter*), or at least publicly named and shamed. Let's just say the Puritan anti-cheating policy made modern prenups look friendly.

- "Fornication" (premarital sex): If an unwed couple was found to be doing more than kissing, the usual sentence was a forced marriage or a fine and public humiliation – sometimes both. They might literally compel the couple to tie the knot, figuring that makes it sort-of okay (after a good whipping to drive the lesson home, naturally). Nothing says romantic wedding like a judge growling "I sentence you two to matrimony, now kiss and make it legal."

- Various other "sins" like gambling, wearing overly fancy clothes, dancing, or even *smoking in public.* Yes, lighting up a cigarette (or pipe, back then) where others could see was a no-no. Puritans were basically the ultimate killjoys – or, put more nicely, they had an intense focus on communal righteousness.

The logic behind all this was that any personal indulgence might invite God's anger on the whole community. One couple kissing could be the little crack that lets Satan slip in and wreak havoc. (In reality, a couple kissing might lead to… a couple more kisses and, who knows, a baby down the line – which in a colonial village is probably a net positive, but try telling them that.) So the Puritans truly believed they were doing God's work by policing hormones and hand-holding.

From our modern viewpoint, it's easy to laugh at how uptight it all was. And we should – it's frankly hilarious that a married man was punished for a peck on the cheek, or that teenagers had to practically court via a speaking tube to avoid temptation. But there's also a familiar ring to it. Haven't we all encountered someone or some institution acting as the "morality police"? Think of certain high schools with ultra-strict dance rules (leave room for the Holy Spirit, kids!), or towns that ban kissing scenes on billboards. The Puritans were just operating at an extreme end of that spectrum.

The universal lesson here is that no matter how much society tries to legislate purity and repress natural attraction, people will find a way to express their feelings – even if it lands them in the stocks. Love (or at least lust) laughs in the face of authority. Every stolen kiss in Puritan New England was basically a teeny rebellion. And every punishment handed down was the authorities' way of saying, "Not on our watch!" This tension – passion versus piety – gives these old stories a relatable spark. We might chuckle, but we also nod: we too chafe at anyone telling us how to love or whom to kiss.

So the next time you hold hands in public or kiss your sweetie on a Sunday, remember poor Thomas Kemble and be grateful you're not in 1650s Boston. Puritan romance was truly an extreme sport, with a high risk of public embarrassment. Yet, despite the stocks and fines, young lovers still sneaked in kisses and secret meetings. In a way, the humor and the heart in these tales come from the oldest story ever – the more forbidden the love, the more tempting it becomes. The Puritans, in trying so hard to prevent any hint of scandal, ended up creating little soap operas in every village. And admit it – we all love a good soap opera, especially one with bonnets, Bibles, and a pair of star-crossed kids caught kissing by the apple barrel.

Jumping the Broom

Meanwhile, in the Antebellum South, there was an entirely different kind of love rogue at work – not breaking the law *by* marrying, but breaking the law by inventing marriage where it wasn't allowed. Enslaved African Americans were denied one of the most basic human rights: the right to legally marry the person they loved. Slaveowners feared that recognizing those bonds would make the enslaved less "property" and more "people" (Heaven forbid they acknowledge their humanity!). Marriage meant family, stability, possibly the audacity to ask not to be sold away from your spouse – all inconvenient for the slave economy. So, no legal marriages for slaves.

You could live with someone as husband and wife in practice, but the law treated you as two single individuals who coincidentally cohabited (until the master decided to sell one of you off, because he could).

But love, as we're seeing, has a way of sprouting even in the harshest soil. Enslaved men and women fell in love and wanted to declare commitment just like anyone else. So they said, "To heck with the law, we'll make our own tradition!" Thus was born the practice of *jumping the broom*. If you've ever attended a Black wedding where the couple leaps over a broomstick at the end of the ceremony, you've seen a beautiful nod to this heritage. But back in slavery days, jumping the broom wasn't a quaint add-on; it was often the entire wedding ceremony.

Here's how it typically worked: The couple (let's call them, say, William and Mary, for any given pair in the 1800s) would gather their community in the slave quarters or some discreet spot. Someone would lay a simple broom on the ground. There might be a bit of whispered prayer or a song – maybe an elder saying a few words of blessing if they were lucky to have one present. Then, hand in hand, the bride and groom would literally jump forward over the broomstick together. On landing, boom – they were considered married in the eyes of their own community. Cue modest celebration: perhaps some clapping, a hug, maybe even secretly sharing a cup of whatever passable drink they had.

No officiant legally sanctioned it, no county clerk recorded it, and certainly no fancy three-tier cake was waiting. But in that jump, their hearts and those watching knew: these two are committing to each other. In a world that claimed they didn't have the right to family or fidelity; they made a sacred promise anyway.

Why a broom? Well, the full origins are a bit murky. There's evidence that broomstick weddings were a thing in parts of West Africa and even among poor peasants in Europe (like in Wales) who couldn't afford a church wedding. The broom might symbolize the home they'd build together – literally, a tool of housekeeping – or the act of sweeping away the old and starting fresh. It also may have simply been something handy and ordinary that could stand in *for* a marriage altar. I like to think it's partially symbolic and partially, "We used what we had, and we weren't allowed church bells or rings, so darn it, we used a broom." DIY to the core. It's kind of poetic: love sweeping two people off their feet, via one quick jump.

These "broomstick marriages" were not without risk or sorrow. Since the slaveholders didn't officially recognize them, any promise of "till death do us part" often had a grim addendum: *"...or until Master sells one of us to a plantation downriver."* Enslaved folks sometimes darkly joked they were married "till death or distance do us part," with distance meaning the heartbreaking day one spouse was sold hundreds of miles away. Imagine saying vows with the knowledge that your family could be torn apart at a whim. It's courage and hope of an extraordinary kind.

And yet, far from being purely mournful, many accounts show that these clandestine weddings were moments of real joy and quiet rebellion. Some slaveowners, especially on larger plantations, actually allowed a bit of ceremony – possibly a calculated move to encourage stable pairings (happy-ish slaves might work harder, they figured), or just because even they had a shred of decency to permit a celebration now and then. There are stories of plantation masters "officiating" in a condescending way, like "By the power vested in me (by me), I pronounce you man and wife – until I say otherwise." Ugh. But the truly meaningful part was always what the enslaved community themselves imbued it with.

We have records from ex-slaves who fondly remembered jumping the broom. One woman recalled how they decorated a room and prepared a feast in secret – as grand as they could make it. Another account described how everyone in the quarters would come to witness, dressed in the best clothes they had (perhaps an old suit jacket handed down from the master, or a dress made from scrap cloth but immaculately clean). For one night, they created their own world where their love was valid and blessed, even if the white world refused to honor it.

Fast forward to 1865: the Civil War ends, slavery is abolished – ding, dong, the wicked institution is dead (legally, at least). Suddenly, those couples who had jumped the broom or simply lived as husband and wife got a chance to legalize their love. And boy, did they line up for it! The Reconstruction era saw an explosion of weddings among freedpeople. In some places, Union Army chaplains or Freedmen's Bureau agents went around gathering couples for mass marriage ceremonies. Imagine the scene: dozens of couples at a time, from elderly pairs who'd been together 40 years to young lovebirds just starting out, all saying "I do" and signing their names (or an X, if they were illiterate) on official marriage certificates. It must have felt like a dream – "We're *really* married now, in the eyes of the law and the Lord, with papers to prove it!"

There are accounts of group weddings so large that one minister married 100 couples in a single day, assembly-line style. "Do you take this woman…?" "I do." "Do you take this man…?" "I do." Next! It was perhaps the busiest Vegas wedding chapel you could imagine, except it was under oak trees in the South with the ink still wet on Emancipation. Some ceremonies were held in chapels or wherever they could fit, and communities threw as much festivity into it as possible – flowers, homemade veils, a banjo or fiddle playing and plenty of tears of joy. After all those years of being told their relationships didn't count, here came the validation. Former slaves often insisted on the whole shebang: the preacher, the ring, the vows in proper form. They craved that sense of equality – to do it like free people do.

Interestingly, while the broomstick ritual itself faded right after slavery (since folks preferred the formal ceremonies they'd been denied), it never disappeared entirely. Black communities passed down the story, and by the 20th and 21st centuries, jumping the broom resurged as a cultural tradition. Now you might see a Black couple jump the broom at their wedding as a loving tribute to ancestors – with a decorated broom, maybe even inscribed with their names. It's a way of saying, "We remember when our love had to leap over injustice – literally."

The spirit of those broom-jumping couples teaches us something profound wrapped in humor and heart: when the powers-that-be said "your love doesn't matter," the lovers essentially replied, "watch us make it matter." They turned a household cleaning tool into a sacred object. Talk about life giving you lemons and you make lemonade…life gave them a broom and they made a wedding.

From a modern perspective, it's as if you were denied a marriage license, so you throw your own wedding on your own terms – maybe with an iPhone officiating via Siri, and you sign a napkin instead of a certificate. It sounds absurd, but it's also beautifully human. We find ways to mark the important moments of life, even if we have to color outside the lines. And in doing so, we often create traditions that last. Love laughs at limitations, again.

So the next time you see newlyweds leap over a broom or hear the phrase "jumping the broom," remember its origins. It's not just a cute Pinterest idea for a rustic wedding. It's a symbol of resilience and defiance, born from a time when loving someone enough to marry them was an act of rebellion for Black Americans. If that isn't both romantic and badass, I don't know what is. Cupid in the colonies sometimes wore chains, but he still found a way to fly over that broom every single time.

'Til Shipwreck Do Us Part

Our final tale takes us to the high seas and the wild frontiers – and into the realm of what we might call colonial bigamy by accident. If you've ever watched a soap opera or a telenovela, you know the classic plot: Beloved Spouse disappears, presumed dead. Grieving Partner eventually moves on and remarries. Surprise! Original Spouse is actually alive and walks through the door one day – *cue dramatic music and a triple take.* Colonial America had this plot happen often enough that it practically needed its own daytime TV slot. And eventually, it even got its own law – known later as "Enoch Arden" laws – to clean up the legal tangle.

But first, imagine being one of the people in this situation around, say, 1700. Let's spin a scenario: John and Abigail, a colonial couple, happily married on a farm in New England. John goes on a sea voyage to trade for some exotic goods (or maybe he joins a whaling crew –

something risky but potentially profitable). He promises Abigail he'll be back in six months. Well, six months pass, no John. A year, no word. Perhaps some debris from a wrecked ship washes ashore, or another sailor comes back and says, "There was a terrible storm; no survivors seen." Our friend Abigail is devastated. All signs point to John being quite dead – swallowed by the merciless Atlantic.

Years go by. Abigail, now technically a widow, eventually finds comfort with someone new – perhaps the local blacksmith, a kind man who helped her with the farm after John's "death." They fall in love (slowly, respectful of dear departed John's memory at first, but love has a way, right?). They marry. The town likely approves; after all, no one expects a woman to live alone forever, and it's nice to see her smile again. Abigail and the blacksmith even have a child together. Life is good, sprinkled with that bittersweet remembrance of past tragedy but a hopeful future.

And then John comes back from the dead. Cue *jaw drop*. It turns out John was not dead at all – perhaps he was stranded on a desert island Cast Away-style, talking to a Wilson-like coconut for company until a passing ship rescued him. Or he was captured by pirates and just escaped. Or he had amnesia (hey, if we're going full soap opera). Whatever the case, he strides into town one sunny afternoon just as Abigail, her new husband, and little baby are coming back from church. Can you imagine the scene? Abigail probably went pale as a ghost; the blacksmith nearly dropped the baby; John's like "Honey, I'm home... What's going on here?!"

In a movie, this is where dramatic music swells. In colonial reality, this is where legal Pandora's box opens. Because now, Abigail has one husband too many. By law, you can only have one – bigamy (being married to two people) is illegal and in those days was actually a criminal offense. But is it really fair to call her a bigamist? She legitimately thought Husband #1 was fish food at the bottom of the ocean when she married Husband #2. The whole community thought so too. It's an accident, but one with huge consequences.

What to do? Colonial laws were not well-equipped for this scenario initially. Generally, the first marriage was still considered valid since the spouse wasn't *really* dead. That would mean her second marriage was null and void the moment John returned. But that's easy on paper, brutal in practice. Abigail has a life with Blacksmith now – maybe she loves him more at this point, and there's a child who calls him dad. And poor John – he survives an odyssey to come home, only to find himself effectively replaced. The emotional carnage here is enormous. It's like *Survivor: Marriage Edition*, where someone's getting voted off the island (or out of the marriage).

Different colonies handled it differently, often as one-off decisions. Sometimes, the returning spouse might agree to quietly depart if they truly wanted the best for their ex. (There's a famous literary example of this selflessness: Lord Tennyson's poem "Enoch Arden" from 1864, which later gave the name to these laws. In it, a shipwrecked sailor returns to find his wife happily remarried with kids. He nobly decides not to reveal himself, essentially letting her remain happy while he slips away brokenhearted. Grab the tissues – it's rough.) But not everyone was as noble as Enoch Arden. Some returnees marched into court and said, "That's my wife/husband, and I want 'em back!" And legally, they often had a point.

Imagine being the judge in such a case. You've got two men claiming the same wife (or vice versa). One has the law on his side (the first marriage), the other has maybe years of cohabitation and even kids on his. If the judge picks the first spouse as the "rightful" one, the second marriage is erased and those kids might be considered illegitimate – a heavy stigma. If he somehow validates the second marriage, what do you do with the first spouse? Tell him "Sorry you were presumed dead; tough luck, bachelorhood for you"? Either way, someone gets hurt, and you're technically endorsing bigamy or adultery in some form. No-win situation, party of three, your table is ready.

In practice, many of these cases ended with the first marriage being restored on paper (since you can't be married to two, the law defaulted to the earliest). The displaced spouse #2 would have their marriage essentially annulled. Sometimes the community would kind of accept the second family quietly anyway, but legally they were in a grey zone. It was messy and tragic all around – fertile ground for gossip, scandal, and general moral confusion in communities that liked things tidy.

By the 18th and 19th centuries, as these scenarios kept popping up (frontier life and sea voyages continued to produce missing persons cases), lawmakers started to codify solutions. The emerging "Enoch Arden laws" basically said, in effect: *If your spouse has been missing without a trace for a certain number of years (often seven was the magic number, borrowed from old British common law ideas), you can legally presume them dead. You're then free to remarry without being considered a bigamist. If the first spouse miraculously returns after that time... well, sorry Charlie (or sorry John), you can't just waltz in and reclaim everything. The new marriage stands.* These laws were a compassionate recognition that people shouldn't have to live in limbo forever, nor be punished for moving on when a tragedy seems certain.

Of course, no law could erase the personal drama. Even with an Enoch Arden statute, imagine the emotional toll. It's the stuff of nighttime drama series: the reappeared husband watching from afar as his wife laughs with her new family on the porch; the wife torn between guilt and relief; the new husband sizing up the old one, both of them wondering who she truly loves. You could base an entire season of *Downton Abbey* or *This Is Us* on one of these cases!

Modern times have equivalents – soldiers missing in action who turn up years later, castaways (rare but it's happened), or even just people who vanish and are declared dead, only to be found alive. Each time it happens, the headlines splash and we all lean in, captivated by the human drama. It strikes at a deep question: *When, and how, do you let go? And* if fate reverses itself, what then?

For colonial America, the lesson was learned through hard experience: sometimes life doesn't fit neatly into church sermons about eternal vows. Sometimes "till death do us part" has an unexpected asterisk: "unless presumed death was an error – in which case, uh, we have some paperwork to sort out." The humorous angle, in hindsight, is how utterly ill-prepared everyone was for these romantic plot twists. No one stood at the altar thinking, "I'll love you forever, unless you disappear in a shipwreck and I marry the cute blacksmith next year." But maybe they should have included a clause!

In a lighter comparison, think of all the rom-coms and sitcoms that play with old flames returning or mistaken deaths. Ross and Rachel's on-and-off in *Friends* has nothing on Colonel William and his two Mrs. Williams of 1750 (fictional example, but surely there were some). At least in modern times we have divorce courts and counseling. In the 1600s and 1700s, they were flying without instruments, making up rules as they went along.

Ultimately, what came out of these shipwreck love triangles is a kind of bizarrely uplifting point: human beings are resilient and resourceful in love. We grieve, we heal, we find love again – and sometimes life surprises us and we have to make tough choices. The colonists stumbled through it, gossiped about it, occasionally legislated it, but they kept on loving despite the risks. They had to sail ships across unknown oceans to find their fortunes, and their spouses accepted that risk too. In a way, every wife or husband who waved goodbye at the docks knew in their heart, "I may never see them again." Some surely had contingency plans ("If I don't return, move on, be happy"), others just crossed their fingers and prayed.

If there's any universal nugget here, perhaps it's this: love is not a straight line. It can be interrupted by forces beyond our control, whether it's a storm at sea or the twists of fate. And when that happens, people will do what they must to keep going – even break a few rules. And if fate then throws a curveball by undoing what was done, well, people will try to handle that with as much grace (or drama) as they can muster. Today, we thankfully have clearer laws (and better communication – a text message from that desert island would solve everything!). But the emotional core – losing love and finding it again – that's timeless.

Having traversed these four stories – from an interracial love literally bound by chains, to kissers in the stocks, to brooms turned altars, and spouses returned from watery graves – what can we say about love, scandal, power and religion in those days (and perhaps in ours)? A few universal marriage lessons jump out:

- Love finds a way, even when laws or conventions say "no." Whether it meant an Irish servant marrying a slave and thumbing her nose at racist rules, or enslaved couples forging their own ceremonies, people in love will creatively defy authority. The heart doesn't consult the law books.

- Excessive rules and repression can't extinguish human passion – they just make the stories juicier. The Puritans tried to micromanage courtship with fines and public shaming, but they ended up with young lovers sneaking around and creating the very scandals they feared. (Note: telling teenagers "don't you dare" has *never* once stopped a teenager in the history of ever.)

- Marriage is both deeply personal and unavoidably social/legal. It's not just about two people's feelings; it's about status, rights, and recognition. That's why it was such a big deal to deny slaves marriage, or to figure out what to do when a "dead" spouse returned. Who you marry (or don't) affected property, children, social order – everything. And it still does, which is why debates on who can marry whom rage on even now. Love is intimate, but marriage can be downright political.

- Communication is key – even beyond the grave (or presumed grave). If only those sailors and frontiersmen could have sent a letter confirming they were alive! It sounds obvious, but so many heartbreaks in our shipwreck tales could be solved by a simple message in a bottle. In modern relationships, we thankfully just have to send a text. The lesson: don't leave your loved ones in limbo if you can help it.

- Every marriage is a roll of the dice. For Nell and Charles, the dice were extra loaded against them, but they rolled them anyway. For our Puritan kissers, they risked punishment for a chance at affection. For the broom-jumpers, they pledged love knowing it could be torn apart. For those who remarried after loss, they took a chance on love again. There's a bravery in that which crosses time. No risk, no reward, as they say.

- Humor helps. Yes, even in the darkest situations, a little humor carries folks through. I like to think that some Puritans chuckled (quietly) about Captain Kemble's misfortune, or that Nell later joked to Charles, "Honey, I love you, but you were literally a *slave* to my love – now I'm figuratively and literally chained to you!" Gallows humor, maybe, but humor nonetheless. It's a coping mechanism that's as timeless as love itself.

In the grand tapestry of American history, these colonial love stories are the quirky, rebellious threads that give it color. They remind us that behind every law, sermon, or scandal sheet headline, there were real people just trying to connect with one another. Love makes people do outrageous things – sometimes that's uplifting, sometimes it's disastrous, and often it's a bit of both.

So as we laugh and gasp at the antics of Cupid's rogues in periwigs and petticoats, let's also toast to the fact that their spirits live on. The next time you see a couple from different backgrounds holding hands, think of Nell and Charles defying 17th-century haters. When you sneak a kiss in public, be glad no one's hauling you to the stocks (and give a nod to those who were). When you attend a wedding where they jump a broom, feel the weight of that joyful tradition born of resistance. And if you ever hear a wild tale of a lost love returning, know that colonial folks went through the same – hearts racing and breaking just as ours do.

Love, power, scandal, religion – it's all intertwined, yesterday and today. The contexts change, but the core drama doesn't. Perhaps that's why these stories still fascinate: we recognize ourselves in them, for all our supposed modern sophistication. In the end, whether it's 1681 or 2025, love makes fools and heroes of us all. And thank goodness for that – it sure does make for some great stories.

Chapter 4

Revolutions and Revelations – 18th to Mid-19th Century Love Quakes

Revolutions and Revelations – 18th to Mid-19th Century Love Quakes

Welcome, dear reader, to a time when love shook the world—literally. If you think messy celebrity divorces and tabloid scandals are a modern invention, the 18th and 19th centuries are here to raise an eyebrow at you. In this era, passion and principle collided in ways that would make even reality TV producers blush. We're about to tour four incredible true tales of love and marriage that rocked society's foundations. Hold onto your powdered wigs and top hats: these love quakes come with revolutions, revelations, and a hefty dose of irreverent humor.

Picture the genteel past: candlelight, formal manners, stiff corsets, and... surprise! Behind that prim facade, people were rebelling in their bedrooms and at the altar. From revolutionary France's flirtation with no-strings divorce, to an Indian widow's wedding that had an entire culture gasping, to an American icon's scandalous second marriage, and even a bizarre British ban on marrying in-laws – it turns out our forebears were as drama-prone as any Hollywood A-lister. Each story below is a rollercoaster of romance and reform, complete with the kind of societal backlash that today would spawn ten thousand tweets of outrage (and probably a trending hashtag or two). So, let's dive in and see what happens when hearts go rogue in a world of rules

Liberty, Equality... and Divorce?

Liberté, Égalité, Fraternité... and Divorce? Bien sûr, mes amis! During the French Revolution, the guillotine wasn't the only thing severing bonds – the revolutionary government decided it was high time to let unhappy couples cut loose too. It's 1792 in Paris: heads are rolling, ideals are flying, and amidst the chaos some enlightened (or maybe just fed-up) lawmakers pass a radical new divorce law. For the first time ever in France, marriage isn't necessarily "till death do us part". In a country where under the old regime you needed an Act of God (or at least the Pope) to escape a miserable marriage, this was a seismic shift. Suddenly, husbands and wives could split up simply because they both *wanted* to. Imagine telling a stodgy aristocrat in 1780 that in a few years both men *and* women would have equal rights to say "Au revoir, mon amour" – they'd probably sputter in their wig and drop their snuffbox in shock.

At first, folks weren't quite sure how to handle this newfound freedom. Some approached it cautiously, like a cat smelling a new catnip toy, while others dove in headfirst. Enter our hero (or depending whom you ask, *anti*-hero): an *enthusiastic* revolutionary citizen who took full advantage of divorce à la française. This enterprising gentleman managed to divorce and remarry six times in one year. Six times! That's not a marriage, that's a marathon. It's basically the 1790s version of speed-dating, except with actual weddings and paperwork. One can only imagine the gossip in Parisian salons: "Mon Dieu, have you heard? Jacques is on wife number *six*; he's collecting marriages like they're Pokémon cards." If social media had existed, this guy would've gone viral as the ultimate wedding crasher of his own weddings. The new divorce law turned marriage into something you could take for a test drive – and some people test-drove it like a teenager with a new sports car, pedal to the metal.

Not everyone was thrilled by these developments, of course. The Catholic Church was clutching its rosary in horror, nobles were aghast at commoners discarding spouses like last season's fashion, and plenty of ordinary folks thought the world had turned upside-down (which, to be fair, it kind of had). But for a glorious moment, revolutionary ideals even entered the bedroom: liberty, equality, and the pursuit of happiness – or at least the pursuit of a happier marriage – reigned supreme. Husbands and wives who had been stuck in lousy arrangements could finally say "I don't" after saying "I do," and they didn't need to fabricate some elaborate farce to do it. No more running off to convents or concocting fake family trees to annul a union; *le divorce* was as simple as mutual agreement or a few broad reasons like "irreconcilable differences" (in very flowery French, of course).

However, as any wild party night eventually meets the rude dawn, the freewheeling divorce fest couldn't last forever. When the initial revolutionary fervor simmered down, a certain Corsican upstart — you might know him as Napoleon Bonaparte, short in stature but tall in ego — took charge. And let's just say, Emperor Napoleon was not about to let marriage be a casual come-and-go affair on his watch. In 1804 he introduced the Napoleonic Code, a comprehensive set of laws that, among other things, put divorce on a much tighter leash. Napoleon essentially said, "Alright mes enfants, fun's over, back to proper family values." Under his rules, you could still technically divorce, but the grounds got narrower than a Paris alley. It was like going from an all-you-can-eat dessert buffet to a strictly set menu. Wives, in particular, found it much harder to initiate divorce unless Monsieur was basically villain-level awful (think: serious crimes or infamous misconduct). The days of "we're just not in love anymore, let's split" were gone; you better have a darn good reason and evidence to boot.

Napoleon's crackdown had an extra dose of irony served on a silver platter. In a plot twist that could make a soap opera writer smirk, Napoleon himself divorced his wife Joséphine in 1809. Yes, the same guy preaching marital permanence gave his own spouse the royal boot when she didn't produce an heir. Apparently, what's forbidden for the goose is perfectly fine for the imperial gander. He basically rewrote the rules to lock everyone else down, then said, "Except me, I'm special." Classic. It's like a celebrity preacher railing against sin on Sunday and getting caught doing exactly that on Monday. Society under Napoleon took a collective sigh and resigned itself: the brief divorce revolution was over, and marital breakup went back to being a clandestine, difficult affair for another few generations.

So what's the takeaway from this French fling with free love (or free un-love)? In true revolutionary fashion, it proved that even age-old institutions like marriage aren't immune to a little shaking up. For a few wild years, personal happiness actually trumped tradition – a notion as incendiary as the Bastille's fall. It was a peek into a future where marriage could be based on choice and fulfillment, not just duty or "because the priest said so." And though old Boney (that's Napoleon) forced everyone back into marital handcuffs for a while, the genie was out of the bottle. The idea that maybe, just maybe, people should have the liberty to correct a matrimonial mistake never really died. (France would eventually bring back divorce for good in the late 19th century, with far less scandal.) In a sense, the French Revolution's divorce experiment was the original "trial separation" between society and its rigid marital norms. And like any dramatic breakup, it came with gossip, excess, a stern parental figure (Napoleon) shutting it down, and a lesson that echoes to modern times: even in the Age of Enlightenment, love and law make for one volatile cocktail.

Widow Wins the Right to Wed

Now let's jump from the gilded halls of Europe to the dustier roads of colonial India in 1856, where another love quake was about to rattle centuries of tradition. Our story begins with a scene straight out of a very twisted fairytale: a child bride, an untimely death, and a society that expected an eleven-year-old girl to live as a mourning widow *for the rest of her life*. Yes, you read that correctly — Kalimati was 11 years old, and already a widow. In mid-19th century Hindu society, if fate (or rather, awful social customs) dealt you this hand, you were essentially doomed to perpetual mourning. Remarry? *Impossible!* Widows were supposed to wear white, renounce earthly pleasures, and basically vanish into the background like ghostly accessories to the dearly departed. Love, companionship, a second chance at happiness — sorry, not in the script. The caste and conservative religious norms of the time had spoken: a woman's marriage was literally *once in a lifetime*, even if that lifetime ended at puberty. Harsh.

Enter Ishwar Chandra Vidyasagar, a scholarly gentleman with a heart of gold and a spine of steel. Think of him as a cross between a social justice warrior and the most persuasive librarian you've ever met. By day, he was a brilliant Sanskrit pundit and educator; by night, he was plotting how to karate-chop through patriarchal customs (using knowledge as his weapon, not actual karate, but you get the idea). Vidyasagar looked at young widows like Kalimati and thought, "This is absurd and downright cruel." He probably got a lot of side-eye and "know your place" lectures from the traditionalists, but our man Ishwar had a secret power-up: the British were in charge of India's laws at that point, and he was determined to convince the colonial government to legalize widow remarriage. Picture an academic with the passion of a superhero, lobbying crusty officials and citing ancient scriptures like receipts to prove his point. He basically said, "Hey, even our old Sanskrit texts aren't as uptight as you guys. Let the poor widows marry again!" It was a major reformist flex in a time when sticking your neck out could get you socially ostracized or worse.

After tireless campaigning (and probably many exasperated chai breaks), Vidyasagar succeeded in pushing through the Hindu Widows' Remarriage Act of 1856. Cue the dramatic drum roll – because now it was show time to practice what he preached. Just a few months after the law passed, Vidyasagar arranged the first legal remarriage of a Hindu widow under the new Act. And guess who the bride was? Our very own Kalimati, age 11, who finally got to trade in her widow's whites for a wedding sari. The lucky groom was a young man named Shrishchandra Vidyaratna. (No pressure, Shrishchandra – you're just making *history* here, hope you didn't forget the ring!). On December 7, 1856, the wedding took place in Calcutta, and it was far from a quiet family affair. Think of it as part wedding, part political protest, part high-security event. They actually had to hold the ceremony under strict police protection, because hordes of angry orthodox folks were ready to riot at the idea of a widow finding happiness again. Imagine needing a security detail at your wedding not because Beyoncé is performing, but because people literally want to stop the wedding itself. Talk about drama.

As the ceremony went on, conservative Hindu priests and elders practically lost their minds. It was as if someone announced that gravity was cancelled – complete disbelief and outrage. How dare a widow, that too a Brahmin girl, remarry? Caste tradition was being tossed aside like yesterday's newspaper, and the self-appointed guardians of culture were fuming. They shouted, they protested, some probably performed ritualistic curses (we can only speculate). In the streets, the backlash got so intense it sparked skirmishes and near-riots. Think of the most over-the-top reactionary response, multiply it by ten, and you're close. It's the 1856 equivalent of an internet comment section on fire, except with actual fires and brickbats. For many orthodox Hindus, this wedding wasn't just a marriage; it was an assault on the natural order of things, akin to suggesting that the sun should rise in the west or that tea should be brewed *after* adding milk (perish the thought!).

But guess what? The wedding went ahead and Kalimati became a wife for the second time in her very short life – this time with society's (or at least the law's) blessing. Vidyasagar, likely with tears of joy in his eyes and maybe a few singed eyebrows from all the fiery backlash, had won this round. The widow remarriage law and that first courageous wedding were a sucker-punch to the jaw of regressive norms. It signaled that compassion and common sense could team up to defeat even centuries-old customs. And here's a juicy tidbit: Vidyasagar didn't stop at helping strangers. He later married off his own son to a widow, just to silence anyone who dared say he wasn't personally invested in the cause. Talk about putting your money (and your family) where your mouth is.

The tale of Kalimati and her second chance at love (or at least at a normal life) is both heartwarming and head-spinning. Heartwarming because an innocent girl got her life back. Head-spinning because of the sheer level of uproar a simple act of *remarriage* caused. We're reminded that sometimes the bravest acts are as personal as saying "I do" when the world tells you "don't you dare." The universal lesson? Love – and basic human dignity – often need champions to cut through the layers of fear and superstition. And progress usually arrives escorted by scandal and outrage, like a bride with a very unruly entourage. In modern terms, Kalimati's wedding was like a viral post challenging a toxic trend – it got hate, it got love, and ultimately it sparked a conversation that couldn't be silenced. Today, widow remarriage (and hey, marriage in general) is nobody's business but your own, at least legally speaking. For that, we can thank pioneers like Vidyasagar who, in 1856, proved that even a stubborn society can budge when hit by the right mix of logic, courage, and a dash of defiance.

The Abolitionist's "I Do" 2.0

Our next stop on this romantic romp through history brings us to Washington, D.C., in the year 1884. The stage is set for a love story that has "historic plot twist" written all over it. Starring in this tale is Frederick Douglass, the famed formerly enslaved man turned abolitionist, orator, writer, and literal icon of the 19th century. By this point Douglass is in his late 60s, a widower after the death of his beloved wife of 44 years, Anna. You'd think society might cut the man some slack in his personal life given all he'd accomplished (writing bestsellers, advising presidents, fighting for freedom and equality, no biggie). But nah – when Frederick Douglass decided to say "I do" a second time, he inadvertently lit the fuse on one of the era's biggest social fireworks.

Here's what went down: Douglass fell in love with Helen Pitts, a white woman about 20 years his junior. Helen was no random person in his life – she was a progressive feminist, college-educated (a Mount Holyoke alumna, thank you very much), and had worked with Douglass as his secretary at the Recorder of Deeds office. In short, she was a friend, intellectual companion, and shared Douglass's passion for equality. Sounds lovely, right? Two like-minded souls finding each other? Well, hold on to your top hat. In 1884 America, a Black man marrying a white woman was about as scandalous as a headline could get. We're talking societal shockwave. The fact that Douglass was famous only made it a bigger spectacle – imagine if a revered civil rights leader today married someone that sent Twitter into a meltdown; that's the level we're at. This wasn't just any interracial marriage; this was essentially *the* interracial marriage that everyone had an opinion on.

When news of the Douglass-Pitts union got out, just about everybody lost their collective minds. White high society gasped into their smelling salts. Many white Americans who respected Douglass's achievements still balked at the idea of him as a son-in-law. (Helen's own family, abolitionists in principle, were reportedly not thrilled at first about her new Black husband – progressive until it gets personal, huh?). Meanwhile, some Black communities were also taken aback or even displeased, worried that Douglass marrying a white woman could be seen as a rejection of Black women or used as propaganda by racists. Even Douglass's adult children had mixed feelings – their mother had only been gone a couple of years, and now Dad's remarried to someone younger than them and of a different race. You could practically hear the armchair psychoanalysis: "Was he lonely? Was he making a political point? Is this love or a midlife – scratch that – late-life crisis?" The poor guy couldn't even fall in love without everyone and their cousin weighing in.

Through the din of public gossip and editorial screeds, Douglass and Helen remained pretty darn dignified. They understood the hullabaloo but basically said, *your problem, not ours.* Douglass had faced down angry mobs and slave catchers; a few pearl-clutching society types weren't going to intimidate him. When reporters asked Douglass about the controversy, he delivered one of the slickest clapbacks of the century. He pointed out that his first wife, Anna, had been Black – "the color of my mother" – and Helen was white – "the color of my father." In one stroke, he reminded everyone that he was the product of a mixed parentage (his father likely a white man) and implied that *love knows no color.* Boom. Drop the mic, Fred. Douglass basically told the world that he'd marry whomever he darn well pleased, and that true equality meant personal choices were off-limits to society's prejudices. It was the 19th-century equivalent of saying "stay mad" to the haters.

Let's take a moment to appreciate Helen Pitts Douglass, too. She wasn't some passive bride in this; Helen was a fierce advocate for women's rights and racial equality herself. You might say she was "woke" before it was cool (or even a word). She knew exactly what storm they were stepping into by getting married. In fact, when a neighbor quipped, "What will people say?" Helen coolly replied, "Love came to me, and I was not afraid to marry the man I loved because of his color." Talk about a power couple – these two were the real deal, united in more than just romance. They had to be, considering even the White House under President Chester Arthur wagged a disapproving finger at them (Arthur was friendly with Douglass but supposedly called the marriage a "mistake"). If Helen and Frederick had Instagram back then, their hashtag might be #LoveWins – with a side of #DealWithIt.

The Douglass marriage was far more than juicy gossip; it became a symbol and a litmus test. It forced people to confront their own prejudices. Here was one of America's greatest self-made men, a champion of justice, essentially saying, "If you truly believe in liberty and equality, put it into practice and respect my marriage." It was an uncomfortable mirror for a society that prided itself on progress yet recoiled at a Black-white love story. Over time, many came around to accept or at least quiet down about the Douglass-Pitts union. They lived out the rest of Douglass's life as partners, and by all accounts, they were happy together. They even honeymooned in Europe to avoid the initial frenzy – a strategic getaway if there ever was one.

So, what's the modern resonance of this 1884 love quake? In an age where interracial marriages (and many other once-scandalous pairings) are increasingly common, it's easy to forget how brave this couple was just to follow their hearts. They faced down basically *all* the haters of their time. Their story reminds us that social progress isn't just forged in courtroom battles or parliamentary debates; sometimes it's forged at a dining room table where an unlikely couple sits together, defying everyone's expectations by simply being in love.

Douglass and Helen's marriage said, "We are equal, and our love is equal, no matter what you think." That's a message as relevant now as it was then – whether it's about race, gender, or any other barrier love dares to cross. And hey, if an elderly widower and a feisty feminist can shake up the world just by saying "I do," there's hope for the rest of us hopeless romantics with a cause.

You Can't Marry Your Dead Wife's Sister!

For our final tale, let's mosey over to Victorian Britain, where we encounter one of the most bizarre marriage taboos ever written into law – a prohibition so oddly specific it sounds like the setup to a Monty Python sketch. Namely: in 19th-century England, a man was forbidden from marrying his deceased wife's sister. Yes, you read that correctly. Your wife kicks the bucket, and you happen to find solace in the arms of her lovely, helpful sister who's been caring for your kids – a logical and heartwarming scenario by modern standards (Hallmark would make a Christmas movie out of it). But Victorian law said "Nope, that's incest (sort of) and we shan't allow it!" To which many people responded, "Wait… what? She's not my sister. She's not even a blood relative. How is this incest, exactly?" Welcome to the wacky world of affinity laws, where your in-laws are treated like blood kin in the eyes of the church. The idea came from a particular interpretation of the Bible and church law that basically extended the "one flesh" concept of marriage to mean your spouse's family becomes yours. So, in their view, marrying your sister-in-law was akin to shacking up with your actual sibling – a big no-no. The result? Countless grief-stricken widowers and compassionate sisters-in-law had to put their wedding plans on hold for, oh, about five decades while Parliament sorted this out.

Now, Victorian debates in Parliament could be dry, but the Deceased Wife's Sister saga was anything but. It became a perennial hot topic, fueling fiery sermons, scandalized newspaper editorials, and presumably some very awkward family discussions. ("Darling, I know your sister has been wonderful helping with the children… but whatever you do, don't fall in love with her, we'd be pariahs!") The whole issue basically pit the champions of personal choice and common sense against the guardians of religious moral order. On one side were reformers saying, "Look here, isn't it better for the kids and everyone if the widower can marry the auntie who already loves them? How is that worse than him marrying a total stranger? Get over your weird taboo!" On the other side were clergymen and conservatives shrieking, "Think of the family purity! It's tantamount to incestuous depravity! Society will collapse!" If this sounds a bit like those melodramatic debates in movies where one guy yells "It's about principle!" and the other yells "It's about people's lives!", you're not far off. The Victorian public ate it up – this controversy dragged on through the 1800s, kind of like the longest-running soap opera. It was the *"Will they or won't they?"* of its day – except the "they" was the British Parliament and the question was whether they'd ever let a man marry his favorite sister-in-law.

How crazy did it get? The Deceased Wife's Sister Bill was introduced and shot down more times than a game of Whack-a-Mole. It became a running joke that every few years some poor optimistic lawmaker would bring it up again, prompting the House of Lords to clutch their pearls and veto it with gusto. From 1849 onward, the bill was brought up at least 19 times in the House of Commons (where it often passed because common sense apparently had a few friends there) only to be stymied elsewhere, especially by the Lords. The opponents painted doomsday scenarios: Allow this and soon men will want to marry their mothers-in-law, their cousins, their pet iguanas (slippery slope alert!). Meanwhile, supporters pointed out the rank hypocrisy at play. After all, marrying your first cousin was totally legal and actually rather common among the aristocracy (yes, looking at you, Queen Victoria – she married her cousin Albert). So blood relatives marrying? Fine. But a non-blood relative who just happens to be your late wife's sis? Scandal! The inconsistency was rich. It's like saying you can eat chocolate cake for breakfast but oh no, hands off that harmless muffin, that's *immoral*. A lot of everyday folks just didn't buy the church's logic. And indeed, many couples simply found ways around it. Some widowers quietly cohabitated with their sisters-in-law and dared the law to intervene. Others hopped over to places like Scotland or even as far as Australia to tie the knot, since outside of England the rules were laxer. Imagine planning your wedding and thinking, "Hmm, do we invite Aunt Mildred and, by the way, should we hold the ceremony 10,000 miles away so it's actually legal?" Talk about destination weddings with a purpose!

So how did this bonkers ban finally end? Drumroll: The Deceased Wife's Sister Act was passed in 1907. By then King Edward VII was on the throne, and society had chilled out *just enough* to let this law squeak through. It certainly helped that over in the vast British Empire, many colonies had already ditched the ban, and the sky hadn't fallen. (In fact, the Mother Country was starting to look a bit old-fashioned and prudish, and if there's one thing the British hate, it's losing face by being the uncool ones at the imperial party.) After decades of relentless campaigning – seriously, some of these reformers spent their entire careers on this single issue – the opposition finally caved or aged out. The Act allowing widowers to marry their deceased wives' sisters got the royal assent, and at long last, love triumphed over ridiculous bureaucracy. I like to imagine a collective cheer going up from the ghosts of all those thwarted Victorian couples, as well as a few living ones who immediately sent out wedding invitations like "Guess what, it's finally happening!"

The "You can't marry your dead wife's sister" saga might seem comical now, but it highlights a timeless tug-of-war: traditional values versus personal freedom. Today, the idea of banning such a marriage sounds absurd (half of you are probably still stuck on "wait, that was a thing?!"). But to Victorians, it was a hill many were bizarrely ready to die on. Every generation has its version of the Deceased Wife's Sister debate – something that seems vital and moral at the time, and later generations facepalm and wonder what the big fuss was. The lesson here? Love and logic usually get the last laugh, even if it takes a while. And maybe, just maybe, lawmakers should spend less time inventing weird hypotheticals about iguana marriages and more time trusting adults to know whom they want to marry. In the end, sanity prevailed, the empire didn't crumble, and British gentlemen could finally say, "Yes, I *will* marry my favorite sister-in-law, thank you very much," without getting hauled off to jail or hellfire. Progress!

Epilogue: Love's Timeless Tremors

As the dust settles on these tales of matrimonial mayhem, a clear pattern emerges: love and marriage are never just personal affairs – they're tightly interwoven with the culture, laws, and power structures of their time. Whenever someone tries to break the mold, society quakes. But those tremors, those "love quakes," are exactly what push humanity forward. Liberty, equality… and divorce showed that even in an age of revolution, the right to exit a marriage was the next frontier of freedom (and that some people will always overdo a good thing – six divorces, really?). A child widow's remarriage in India proved that compassion can defeat cruel tradition, even if you need an army of arguments and actual police to get there. Frederick Douglass and Helen Pitts's love laughed in the face of prejudice, making a Black and white union a powerful beacon of progress. And the long-winded battle over marrying your dead wife's sister? It taught us that what one era deems scandalous or "unnatural" might later just get a shrug and a "Who cares?"

These stories might be set in cobblestoned streets and candlelit parlors, but their spirit is familiar. We still grapple with who can marry whom, what love should look like, and who gets to decide. The good news is, thanks to these pioneers of passion, we've knocked down a lot of silly barriers. Divorce nowadays is fairly routine (though maybe try not to collect six in a year, okay?). Widows (and widowers) can remarry as they please – and at an appropriate, grown-up age, one hopes. Interracial marriages are celebrated in many places, recognized for the beauty of two cultures coming together. And as for in-law marriages, if that's your thing and everyone's a consenting adult, the law isn't about to stop you (your family Thanksgiving might get weird, but legally you're golden).

Ultimately, what resonates across time is this: love is a force of nature and a force for change. It's been challenging norms and toppling barriers since forever. People in every era find ways to follow their hearts, and in doing so, they often nudge the world toward a more open, understanding place. Sure, there will always be those clutching their pearls, writing angry letters to the editor (or tweets) about "the end of society as we know it." But if history teaches us anything, it's that society *as we know it* is always evolving – usually for the better – and love is often the instigator of that evolution.

So here's to the troublemakers of love, the scandalous sweethearts, and the reformers with a romantic streak. They remind us not to take our modern freedoms for granted. The next time you hear someone say "love conquers all," remember these stories – love not only conquers, it occasionally upends kingdoms, rewrites laws, and gives stodgy lawmakers headaches. And thank goodness for that. After all, a world where love never caused a scandal or a stir would be dreadfully dull, indeed. Now, go hug your spouse (or your sister-in-law, if that's your situation – no judgment here!). The journey to today's "happily ever after" was a wild one, and we're all beneficiaries of those bold hearts from the past.

Chapter 5

Victorian Era & Global Romantics – Class, Empire, and Polygamy Problems

The Commoner and the Crown

Picture this: a fancy Victorian ballroom, all satin and snobbery, when in walks Archduke Johann of Austria with gasp a woman who isn't remotely royal. In fact, she's the local postmaster's daughter. Yes, you read that right – an Archduke and a mailman's kid, strolling in like it's the most natural thing in the world. If Hallmark had existed in 1829, they'd have greenlit this script in a heartbeat. It's basically Cinderella in reverse: instead of a prince searching for a mystery princess, we've got a prince (well, Archduke) openly swooning over a commoner. And the royal family? They absolutely lost their collective minds.

Johann's beloved was Anna Plochl, a bright-eyed, down-to-earth girl who probably had zero training in curtsying to emperors but could sort the heck out of a mail sack. The Habsburg court (think of them as the original ultra-exclusive country club) was scandalized. An imperial Archduke marrying *her*? Cue the pearl-clutching. We're talking full-on Victorian meltdown – smelling salts, fainting couches, and frantic fan fluttering galore. It just wasn't done. Royals were supposed to marry other royals or at least someone with a *von* or *de* in their name, not the neighbor's kid.

But love, that cheeky little rebel, doesn't care about titles. Archduke Johann tried the polite route first: he asked his big brother, the Emperor, for permission to marry Anna. Initially Emperor Franz was like, "Well, okay... on second thought, nope!" He changed his mind faster than a debutante changes dresses. The answer was a firm "Not happening." Johann, however, was determined (love makes stubborn fools of the mighty too). He basically said, "I'm gonna marry her, with or without the crown's blessing." This was the 19th-century equivalent of a royal mic drop.

The compromise? For a while, the court pretended Anna was Johann's "housekeeper." Yes, you heard that euphemism correctly. They literally had to act like this woman — whom he'd been head-over-heels for since she was a teenager — was just there to dust the palace and alphabetize his scrolls. Wink wink, nudge nudge. It was all very "don't ask, don't tell." Victorian PR at its finest: as long as no one *officially* called her his wife, the aristocracy could pretend everything was proper.

After nearly a decade of this charade, the Emperor finally caved in 1829. Perhaps he realized Johann would stay single forever rather than marry some duchess he didn't love. Or maybe Franz just got tired of the gossip and said "Fine, do what you want, I'm over it." So Johann and Anna had a quick, quiet wedding — no lavish spectacle, just a speedy "I do" probably done at midnight with the curtains drawn. This was no royal extravaganza; it was more like eloping in Vegas, but with fewer Elvis impersonators and more Latin prayers.

Even then, the Emperor slapped on conditions. The marriage was what they called *morganatic.* That's a fancy term meaning Anna got to be the Archduke's wife, but she and their future kids were basically disowned from the dynasty. No fancy titles (at first), no succession rights, no invitations to the imperial family's Christmas bash. "Sure, marry your love," the Habsburgs said, "but don't expect to bring her to high tea with Queen Victoria." Eventually they tossed Anna a bone and made her a Baroness so she wouldn't completely embarrass the family at parties. Their son got a title too (Count of Meran – cute, right?), but still, the message was clear: *marry for love, pay the price.*

Yet, despite all the drama and snide whispers, Johann and Anna lived happily enough. She didn't magically turn into a pumpkin or bring down the empire. In fact, their love story quietly nudged the aristocracy forward a smidge. It was like a preview of things to come. Fast forward a century and royals marrying commoners becomes almost trendy (hello, Prince William and Kate Middleton!). Johann's scandalous move showed that marrying outside the golden circle wasn't the end of the world. The sky didn't fall. If anything, the Habsburgs got a beloved folk hero story out of it — the Archduke who followed his heart.

The takeaway? Sometimes the crown sits heavier on a lonely head. Even in an era obsessed with class and rank, a royal guy went "You know what, I choose love." And isn't that the most epic royal rebellion? It's the Victorian version of *"Love conquers all, now hold my beer (or rather, my champagne)"*.

Empire Crossing Hearts

Now let's leave Europe's gilded cages and venture into the wild landscapes of the British Empire, where Cupid was sneaking around shooting arrows across color lines — oh my! The British liked to think they were spreading "civilization" (by that they meant afternoon tea and pith helmets) to every corner of the globe. But lo and behold, along with the Union Jack, British lovebirds sometimes crossed cultural divides in scandalous fashion.

Picture a proper Victorian lady, all corseted and parasol'd, arriving in sunny South Africa. She's supposed to be the prim & proper example of British womanhood abroad. Instead, she falls head over heels for a local king. Yes, I'm talking about Princess Susie "Sunni" Reynolds — an honest-to-goodness aristocrat (nicknamed "Princess" by society wags) with a rebellious streak — who in 1898 did the unthinkable: she married King Sekhukhune, a South African chief. Imagine the collective spit-take of the British upper crust. The gossip mills would've churned out headlines like: *"Society Lady Elopes with African King! Queen Victoria Not Amused!"*

Sunni wasn't your average debutante. While other girls were playing piano and sipping Earl Grey, she was out exploring the savannah (much to her chaperone's horror). Let's say she met Sekhukhune at a colonial gathering — one glance, and sparks flew. Next thing you know, she's trading her lace gloves for a wedding ring and a life in his homeland. Their ceremony must have been a sight. On one side, the bride's British relatives, red-faced in stuffy wool suits under the blazing sun. On the other, Sekhukhune's people in vibrant dress, eyeing these pale, overdressed in-laws with curiosity. Awkward glances all around? You bet. It's *Meet the Parents*, empire edition.

Predictably, many back home had a meltdown. Victorian society had a serious case of racial snobbery, and an interracial marriage in high society was beyond taboo. In gentlemen's clubs from London to Calcutta, monocles plopped into teacups amid gasps of "What's the empire coming to?" If Victorian Twitter existed,

#SunniAndSekhukhune would have trended for weeks with equal parts outrage and fascination. Even Queen Victoria, ruler of a multicultural empire (from a very safe distance), likely did a double take at this love story.

British newspapers likely had a field day describing this "princess gone rogue" and her "savage chief" (Victorian tabloids were *anything* but subtle). In Sekhukhune's land, people probably just shrugged and joked that their king had a taste for imported goods. Each side spun its own dramatic version of the tale, but the couple themselves were busy living it.

As for Sunni's posh family back in England, they presumably needed a stiff drink (or five) to swallow this development. I wouldn't be surprised if her father threatened to disown her one minute, then bragged to his friends the next that his daughter was a queen in Africa. High society has a funny way of coming around when it suits them.

Meanwhile, the newlyweds just got on with life, learning each other's ways. I imagine Sunni cheerfully picking up her new family's language, and Sekhukhune gamely enduring the occasional afternoon tea for her sake. Sure, they'd have cultural mix-ups — she might find his people's dances wild yet exhilarating; he might find English cooking hilariously bland — but they made it work, day by day.

And they weren't alone. Across the empire, other love rebels defied the color lines. In India, back in the East India Company days, some British officers "went native" and married Indian princesses or commoners (scandalous even then). By Victoria's time, the establishment frowned on such unions, but a few daring couples still fell for each other and tied the knot. These pairs weathered gossip, side-eye, even exile, yet persisted — living proof that the heart doesn't heed the imperial rulebook. In a way, Sunni and Sekhukhune pulled a Meghan-and-Harry long before that was cool (or remotely acceptable). Every interracial union poked a tiny hole in the balloon of colonial pretension.

By simply loving whom they loved, these couples made people confront their prejudices. The empire adored its order and hierarchy, but love cheerfully messed all that up. Consider it a win for humanity over hubris: love 1, empire 0.

One Man, Many Wives – The Mormon Matrimony Mess

While Victorians in London fussed over who one should marry, over in America folks were arguing over how *many* one could marry. That's right — welcome to the wild world of 19th-century Mormon polygamy, basically the craziest season of *The Real Housewives of Utah* never filmed. You thought one mother-in-law was a handful? Try juggling a dozen wives (and their mothers) and you've got a full-blown circus.

In the mid-1800s, the Mormon Church settled in Utah and openly practiced plural marriage. The logic was something like, "Hey, biblical patriarchs had multiple wives, so why can't we?" Enter Brigham Young, Mormon leader and overachiever in the matrimony department. This guy had fifty-five wives — yes, 5-5, no typo — and around fifty-seven kids. Imagine the family reunions. Actually, imagine the breakfast buffet; he probably needed a dining hall just to seat everyone. Keeping track of birthdays and anniversaries must have required a ledger the size of the Bible. It's funny to picture Brigham juggling dates and names (hello, disaster if he mixed up Mary and Marie), but for the women involved it wasn't all laughs. Sharing a husband is not the romantic dream Jane Austen sold them. Jealousy and drama were inevitable, and coordinating domestic life in a polygamous household was a logistical nightmare. Think color-coded chore charts and an early version of Google Calendar (on paper, of course).

The U.S. federal government, meanwhile, was *not* amused by this marital mayhem. To monogamous mainstream America, Mormon polygamy looked like a perversion of marriage — the 19th-century equivalent of a scandalous viral trend. Newspapers ran lurid cartoons of bearded geezers with harems; preachers thundered from pulpits about "heathens in Utah." Basically, the rest of America said, "One nation under God, not one nation under God *with a dozen sister-wives.*" So Uncle Sam strapped on his boots to play sheriff.

From the 1860s on, new laws banned bigamy and by extension polygamy. Federal marshals literally hunted down polygamist husbands. (Cue a Wild West poster: *Wanted for Having Too Many Wives.*) There were raids and arrests; some men went into hiding or fled the country to dodge prison for the crime of "too much family." They couldn't easily nab Brigham Young himself (he was basically Utah's emperor by then), but plenty of his associates got busted. Congress even dissolved the Mormon Church's corporate status and seized its assets at one point, just to prove they meant business. Utah was told flat-out: "no statehood until you guys quit collecting wives like trading cards."

Finally, by 1890, the church waved the white flag. The Mormon president (Wilford Woodruff, Brigham's successor) issued the famous "Manifesto" saying in essence, "Okay, fine, we'll stop marrying multiple women. Pretty please let Utah become a state now." It worked.

Utah gained statehood in 1896 after officially renouncing polygamy. The existing plural marriages were quietly phased out or allowed to fade away (no new wives, but they didn't exactly kick the old ones out). The great Mormon marital musical-chairs game came to an end — at least publicly.

Of course, polygamy didn't vanish without a trace. A few stubborn groups snuck off to Mexico or Canada where U.S. law couldn't reach, determined to keep their alternative lifestyle alive. Others went deep underground in remote desert towns. (Their descendants pop up on reality TV once in a while, because history has a wicked sense of humor.) Meanwhile, the mainstream LDS Church did a complete about-face — basically like that friend who had a bizarre phase in college and now insists it never happened. "Polygamy? Us? Never heard of her!" (Just ignore those old family photos with great-great-grandpa and his 3 brides.)

The whole polygamy saga raised a question that isn't so foreign today: what defines a marriage, and who gets to decide? In the 19th century, the debate was over one man marrying many women — and it drove the nation to distraction. (Later eras would have different battles over marriage, but that's another story.) The Victorian takeaway here? Even in a buttoned-up age, people were pushing the boundaries of "acceptable" relationships and others were freaking out about it. Some things truly never change.

Married Women, Free at Last

Marriage in the Victorian era wasn't all romance and rebellion; for many women it was practically a hostage situation (minus the ransom notes). The moment a blushing bride said "I do," she effectively disappeared legally. Under the old doctrine of *coverture*, a wife's identity was "covered" by her husband's. She couldn't own property, sign a contract, or even keep her own wages. Legally, she and her hubby became "one person," and spoiler alert — that person was the husband. It was like a magic trick where the magician (Mr. Husband) makes his assistant (Mrs. Wife) vanish into thin air. Poof! Goodbye, legal existence. Hello, life of asking your dear spouse for an allowance to buy pincushions.

By the mid-1800s, women were understandably fed up with playing legal ghosts. A posse of early feminists and allies launched a campaign to exorcise the laws of coverture. Leading the charge were firebrands like Elizabeth Cady Stanton and Ernestine Rose in the U.S., who teamed up with others to tell lawmakers, "Hey, wives are people too." They organized conventions, penned pamphlets, and petitioned state assemblies with the tenacity of today's online activists (only with quill pens and bonnets). These ladies weren't asking for the moon — just the radical notion that a married woman should control her own money and property. Cue the gasps! Many men in power balked. Some warned that giving women rights would *destroy marriage* as everyone knew it. (Translation: they feared a world where wives might say "no" once in a while or, gasp, have their own bank accounts.) One worried politician claimed that if wives could own property, it would "unsex" them — whatever that meant. Probably that women would suddenly grow beards and start acting like men, which of course didn't happen when the reforms finally passed.

Speaking of reforms, change did come — slowly but surely. In New York, 1848, lawmakers passed a Married Women's Property Act letting wives keep property and earnings in their own name. This was huge: a wife in New York could finally inherit a cow from her father without her husband immediately trading said cow for a new plow (or a round of drinks at the tavern). Other states followed suit through the 1850s–1870s, each chipping away at coverture. Across the pond, Britain caught up later; the big breakthroughs were the Married Women's Property Acts of 1870 and 1882. By the 1880s, an English wife could finally say, "Hands off my dowry, dear, it's legally mine!" She could even take a dishonest merchant to court on her own. It was like the universe handed married women a permission slip to be real adults.

This quiet legal revolution changed married life fundamentally. The home was still the home, but the wife within it was no longer legally akin to a child or a piece of furniture. Imagine the dinner table conversations after these laws passed — husbands grumbling that their wives had "lawyered up," and wives smiling because they could finally buy property or stash away savings without needing hubby's okay. (Perhaps Queen Victoria herself sputtered into her tea; she famously called the push for women's rights a "wicked folly," even as she enjoyed ultimate power as a monarch. Irony, thy name is Victoria.)

So what's the big takeaway from all these Victorian love-and-law sagas? Simply this: marriage is never just about two people making googly eyes at each other — it's a mirror of society's values, struggles, and evolutions. In an era known for prim manners and stuffy decorum, we've seen an Archduke defy class rules for love, an aristocrat and an African chief challenge racial barriers, a community in Utah stretch the definition of marriage to its limit, and women everywhere fight to be seen as persons, not property, in their marriages. Each story was a battle against the status quo, and collectively they nudged the world forward (often while providing grade-A gossip material).

The Victorian era may wear a reputation for strictness and propriety, but clearly it was full of rule-breakers with their hearts and minds set on change. Love and courage made people do scandalous, wonderful things — and thank goodness for that. What was outrageous in 1850 became merely eyebrow-raising by 1900, and many of those once-scandalous changes laid the groundwork for the freedoms we take for granted today. The universal lesson here? When it comes to marriage, fights for love or for fairness can rattle even queens and governments — but in the long run, passion and progress usually prevail. History is basically one long series of "happily ever after… eventually." And if the Victorians taught us anything, it's that a little irreverence and a lot of persistence can transform society — one wild romance at a time.

Chapter 6

Love in War and Upheaval – Early 20th Century Shake-Ups

No Crown, All Heart

1936, London. King Edward VIII sits on the fanciest throne in the world – but he's got a *huge* problem. See, Eddie (let's call him that for fun) is head-over-heels in love with Wallis Simpson, an American socialite who isn't exactly princess material in the eyes of the British establishment. Why? Well, for starters, she's American (cue *horror movie scream* from the palace aides). Worse, she's been divorced. Twice. In the 1930s British royal rulebook, that's like showing up to high tea in a tracksuit – simply not done.

Edward's advisors and family are losing their collective royal minds. The King dating a twice-divorced American? The Archbishop of Canterbury is clutching his pearls (or rather, his Bible). British high society folk are sputtering into their Earl Grey. The government basically tells the King, *"It's her or the crown, mate. You can't have both."* Imagine that: the ultimate bachelor ultimatum.

Now, if you think modern royals have drama (looking at you, Harry and Meghan), Edward and Wallis were the OG scandalous couple. British newspapers initially keep things hush-hush (stiff upper lip and all), but the American press? Oh, they're all over it like paparazzi on a Kardashian. Newspapers around the world scream about a royal love scandal, and it's the 1936 equivalent of trending on

Twitter – if Twitter existed, #KingQuitsForLove would be blowing up. The British public finally catches on and everyone has an opinion. It's the biggest tea-spill in decades.

Let's break down why Wallis caused such a royal meltdown:

- American Accent: An American accent in Buckingham Palace – the old guard found that about as palatable as cold tea.

- Divorcée Times Two: She had not one but *two* ex-husbands still living. For the Church of England (which the King heads), this was a big nope. (Henry VIII broke England from Rome over a divorce, but apparently a 20th-century king still couldn't marry a divorcée. Irony much?)

- No "Proper" Pedigree: Wallis wasn't royalty or even British aristocracy. To the snobs in royal circles, this was like a commoner crashing the VIP section – *so uncouth!*

Despite all the drama, Eddie is absolutely smitten. Picture him tossing the crown aside like a guy quitting a high-paying job to follow his heart. And that's basically what he does. In a move that rocks the entire British Empire, Edward VIII abdicates – meaning he literally says "I don't wanna be King anymore, cheers!" – so he can marry Wallis. Yes, love wins, and the monarchy loses its darn mind.

He announces on live radio (1936's version of a viral broadcast) that he can't do the job without "the woman I love." In other words: *No Wallis, no crown.* It's a plot twist for the ages – the man gives up ruling an empire for love. It's one for the history books and romance novels.

The aftermath is equal parts romantic and awkward. Edward becomes simply the Duke of Windsor and scurries off with Wallis to live overseas – largely in exile, throwing glamorous parties in France and rubbing shoulders with high society. Britain crowns his stammering younger brother (George VI – the one from *The King's Speech*) as the new monarch. The royal family essentially erases Edward from the family group chat. Wallis Simpson never gets that Queen title, but she *does* get her man – plus an impressive jewelry collection and endless gossip written about her.

The British establishment pretends everything's fine (nothing to see here, just a king tossing away his crown for love, la-di-da). But the story becomes legend. It's the ultimate "love over duty" tale. People either swoon – *"He sacrificed everything for her, how romantic!"* – or shake their heads – *"What an irresponsible chap, nearly caused a constitutional crisis!"*. The tabloids dine out on the scandal for years.

In the end, Edward and Wallis's saga set the bar high for royal drama. They were basically the Meghan and Harry of their day, but on steroids: imagine Harry not just stepping back from royal duties but literally quitting the throne. Edward's choice showed that sometimes even kings can't have it all – no crown, but all heart. And for better or worse, he proved that love can turn even the most blue-blooded life upside down. The British monarchy survived, but they learned a royal lesson: affairs of the heart can rock the mightiest institutions. After all, when a king tosses aside a kingdom for love, it's clear that *no one* is immune to Cupid's chaos.

Free Love Fiasco

Rewind to 1917 in Russia – the Bolsheviks have taken over, and they're not just rearranging the political furniture; they're also eyeing the bedroom and the wedding chapel. Comrade Lenin and crew basically say, "You know those old marriage rules? Yeah, toss 'em." In the chaotic free-for-all after the Revolution, love and marriage become a grand social experiment. It's like the government launched the world's first state-sponsored dating app and everyone's invited to beta test. The motto? *"Free love."* Well... at first.

Right after the revolution, Bolshevik idealists decided marriage was an outdated bourgeois trap. They wanted to liberate love from church, capitalism, and even paperwork. Imagine a society where swiping right isn't needed because the state kind of already did it for you – *"Go forth, comrades, and love as you will!"* Laws were passed to make relationships super flexible:

- No-Fault, No-Hassle Divorce: Breaking up got absurdly easy. One spouse could dump the other via a simple letter – the ex would literally get a "Congrats, you're single!" note in the mail. Yikes.

- Equal Rights (on Paper): Men and women were declared equal in marriage. Great on paper, except some husbands took it as license to abandon their families – not cool, comrade.

- Abortion and Birth Control: They even legalized abortion in 1920 (free in state hospitals), decades ahead of their time – for a while, anyway.

For a brief, heady moment, it's romantic anarchy out there. Young people in the 1920s Soviet Union test their newfound freedoms. Couples shack up without bothering to marry, because why not? Divorce loses its stigma – it's almost trendy. Some folks rack up marriages and breakups faster than a Hollywood starlet in a tabloid decade. Urban legends (and probably some propaganda) claim the Bolsheviks want to "nationalize women" – as if wives would become community property. That wasn't true, but it shows how wild people *think* this experiment is.

Of course, all this free love comes with a dose of chaos. Sure, it's easier to untie the knot, but that also means some men vanish on their families because it's just so darn easy to walk away. Women often bear the brunt – left with kids and no support, wondering if this "liberation" is a one-way ticket to Single-Mother City. Society is in flux, with expectations whiplashing from "stay loyal forever" to "oh well, get a new spouse, no biggie."

Then enters Joseph Stalin – the ultimate party crasher with the worst vibes. By the mid-1930s, Stalin looks around at the romantic mayhem and basically says, *"Што за чертовщина?!"* (That's "What the heck is this?!" in angry Russian). The freewheeling days of state-sanctioned Tinder are over. Stalin brings back family values with a vengeance, like a grim Soviet Cupid with a clipboard. The government's U-turn is so sharp, people get ideological whiplash. Suddenly:

- Divorce Gets Difficult: No more easy-peasy breakups. By 1936, couples have to jump through hoops to split – court hearings, fees, the whole bureaucratic circus. Serial divorcees face steep fines. Basically, the state's saying "Think *really* hard before you uncouple, folks."

- Abortion Banned: That progressive abortion law? Reversed in '36. Stalin needs bodies for factories and the Red Army, so nope – you're having that baby.

- Singles Taxed: Yes, the USSR literally put a tax on being single or childless. Nothing like a little financial incentive to get hitched and start popping out kids.

- Mommy Medals: On the flip side, mothers with a ton of kids get medals. Pump out ten babies and you become a "Heroine Mother" of the Soviet Union. The message: make babies, not free love.

In short, the revolution's love experiment did a full 180. One day it's "free love, go wild," and the next it's "family values or else." The wild party of the 1920s turns into the strict curfew of the 1930s – talk about ideological whiplash.

The Bolsheviks learned the hard way that you can rewrite laws overnight, but you can't rewrite human nature so easily. Hearts don't always follow decrees. Love still found ways to be chaotic, whether or not it had state approval. The free love fiasco proved that romance can be as unruly as ever, no matter how you legislate it. When politics and passion collide, expect a bumpy ride – and maybe keep the vodka handy.

Love Conquers the Führer (Briefly)

Fast-forward to 1943, in the heart of Nazi Germany. The Third Reich is at full throttle being evil, and Hitler's regime has made it pretty clear they're not fans of romance that doesn't fit their racist rulebook. Jewish people are being deported by the thousands, families torn apart. It's one of the darkest chapters in human history – not exactly a rom-com setting. Yet, amid all this terror, an unlikely love-story rebellion is brewing on a street in Berlin.

Picture a cold February morning on Rosenstrasse (that's "Rose Street" – how fitting). Nazi police have rounded up about 2,000 Jewish men married to non-Jewish German women. According to Nazi racial law, these husbands shouldn't even *exist* in Berlin – until then they'd been spared deportation because they had Aryan wives, but now even that slim protection is gone. They're slated for transport to who-knows-where (we know now: concentration camps). The Gestapo locks them up in a building on Rosenstrasse. Most people in Nazi Germany would be petrified into silence. But not these guys' wives. Oh no. These ladies said, "Not today, Hitler."

One by one, then dozens, then hundreds, German wives of the imprisoned men show up at Rosenstrasse, right outside the detention center. They stand there day after day, demanding loudly: *"Give us our husbands back!"* Imagine the scene: a bunch of otherwise ordinary women – housewives, secretaries, mothers – transforming into lionesses defending their mates. They're staring down SS guards with rifles and refuse to budge. It's like the world's most high-stakes sit-in. No permit, no weapons, just sheer wifely determination. Talk about guts – these women are effectively telling the Nazi regime, *"We want to speak to the manager of Nazi Germany!"*

At first, the Gestapo is flabbergasted. This is Nazi Berlin – public protest isn't a thing, especially not by Aryan women on behalf of their Jewish husbands. The propaganda machine has painted Jews as the ultimate villains, yet here are "proper" German ladies basically calling

BS. The crowd swells, hundreds strong, and they keep coming despite frigid weather and the very real risk of being shot or dragged off themselves. When soldiers aim guns and threaten to fire if they don't disperse, the wives shout back, *"Murderers!"* – right to the soldiers' faces. Standing up to armed Nazis and calling them out like that takes some serious spine.

This standoff lasts a week. It's seven days of Nazi bigwigs scratching their heads, unsure if they should massacre a bunch of high-status German housewives in broad daylight. Meanwhile, word of the protest trickles out (even the foreign press gets wind of it). Joseph Goebbels – Hitler's propaganda minister and all-around toady – realizes this is turning into a PR nightmare. The regime that prides itself on total control is being openly defied by *wives*. Loyal German wives, no less, who just want their husbands back. Not a good look for the Führer.

So the unthinkable happens: the Nazis blink first. Goebbels quietly orders the men at Rosenstrasse released. The genocidal Nazi regime actually lets these Jewish husbands go back home to their wives. Some who had already been shipped off to camps are even brought back. It's probably the only time Hitler's government ever said, "Ugh, fine, have it your way," in response to public protest. The women of Rosenstrasse basically cracked the Nazi armor, if only for a moment. Love (and outrage) 1, Hitler 0.

Of course, the regime didn't exactly advertise this defeat on the front page of the newspaper. They swept it under the rug, the war raged on, and the Holocaust's horrors continued unabated. The brave women who stood up were mostly just relieved to hold their husbands again and get the heck away from Rosenstrasse.

Yet that week remains one of those astounding blips in history – a ray of light in a very dark time. Who would've thought a bunch of determined wives armed with nothing but love, grit, and a sharp tongue could outmaneuver the Third Reich? It sounds like a Hollywood script – except it really happened.

The Rosenstrasse protest showed that even a tyrannical government bent on hate can be punctured, however briefly, by courage fueled by love. These women didn't set out to be heroes or freedom fighters; they just wanted their husbands back. In doing so, they proved that you can't break a marriage when one spouse is willing to risk everything to protect the other. In the grand scheme, it was a small victory – but a wildly improbable and inspiring one. For one brief moment, love conquered the Führer – and that's worth a cheer (and maybe a shot of schnapps).

War Brides and I Dos Across Borders

World War II wasn't just victory parades and new world maps – it also sparked an epic international romance fest. By 1945, as the smoke clears, Cupid has been busy on the battlefields. When millions of young men shipped out overseas, a lot of them came back not just with war stories, but with wives. Love knows no borders, and it sure doesn't wait for visas.

All across Europe and Asia, American GIs were falling head over combat boots in love with locals. A farm boy from Kansas meets a pretty London typist in a bomb shelter during the Blitz – boom, they're sharing Hershey bars and planning forever. An infantryman in Occupied Japan shyly courts a Japanese nurse with help from a pocket phrasebook – hearts melt across a language barrier. It's like a worldwide edition of The Bachelor, except the roses are wartime rations and nobody has time for nonsense because the world's on fire.

Cue the culture shock. Many American families had never met anyone from overseas until their sons brought home these foreign brides with their accents, habits, and recipes. Suddenly, Aunt Mildred in Ohio has a British daughter-in-law who insists on afternoon tea instead of coffee, while another GI's Italian wife teaches the family that real spaghetti doesn't come from a can. Meanwhile, a Japanese bride in California is politely trying to understand her new family's obsession with casserole and Jell-O salad. Worlds are colliding in kitchens and living rooms across the country, often to hilarious effect.

Of course, Uncle Sam's laws weren't quite ready for this love invasion. The Immigration Act of 1924 had basically slammed the door on most immigrants. So in 1945, Congress hurriedly passed the War Brides Act, essentially telling immigration, *"Stand down – let these ladies in."* For once, love overruled paperwork.

The arrival of war brides is headline news. Some Americans are fascinated ("Our Johnny married a girl from *where*?!"). Others are suspicious or even racist – "Why's he bringing home *that* girl from overseas?" (Cue the disapproving gossips). But most folks eventually come around when they actually meet these women. Turns out war brides are generally pretty darn charming, determined, and resourceful (surviving a world war tends to build character, who knew?). They learn English, figure out how to navigate American life, and build families that are little cultural melting pots.

In the process, these couples poked holes in a lot of old prejudices. After all, it's hard to hate "foreigners" once your beloved daughter-in-law *is* one – and maybe she's introducing you to Yorkshire pudding or miso soup.

War brides, as a whole, left a legacy. They opened many American minds about interracial and intercultural marriage. In fact, these wartime love stories played a part in changing even the laws. Over time, strict immigration quotas and bans on interracial marriage began to crumble. Love had started rewriting the rules – slowly but surely.

By the time the dust settled, those international "I dos" had changed more than just the lives of the couples. They chipped away at racial barriers and set the stage for a more diverse nation in the decades to come. The War Brides saga is proof that even amid the ugliest of wars, love can plant some pretty beautiful seeds.

Universal Lessons: If there's one thing these wartime love stories teach us, it's that love is the ultimate troublemaker – in a good way. Think about it: a king gave up an empire for it, a revolution tried to rewire it, a group of wives defied a dictator with it, and thousands of GIs broke down borders (and laws) because of it. Love and marriage during times of upheaval turned out to be surprisingly rebellious.

In a way, these stories are a big, bold reminder: from kings to common soldiers, in freedom or under tyranny – the heart wants what it wants. And when the heart wants something badly enough, *no* rule or ruler can stand in its way for long. Marriage – that age-old institution – has an uncanny ability to survive and even thrive in the craziest times by bending the rules or breaking them. So here's to love in the time of upheaval: scandalous, rule-defying, and somehow still finding a happily (or at least *hopefully*) ever after in the mess of history. Because if love can make *that* much mischief and change in wartime, just imagine what it can do in peace.

Chapter 7

Breaking the Color and Age Barriers – Mid-20th Century

The Case of Loving v. Virginia

Once upon a time in 1958, a young couple named Richard and Mildred did something truly outrageous – they fell in love and got married. Scandalous, right? Well, not to most people, but in the Commonwealth of Virginia this was apparently a felony-level offense. Why? Because Richard was white and Mildred was Black, and in those days Virginia acted like a jealous hall monitor for Cupid, enforcing a strict "color within the lines" policy on romance. So when these lovebirds tied the knot (legally, in Washington D.C., where no one batted an eyelash), then came home to Virginia, they woke up one night to find the local sheriff *literally* in their bedroom. No, he wasn't there to deliver belated wedding congratulations – he was there to arrest them for the crime of being an interracial couple peacefully asleep at home. Talk about a rude wake-up call. It's as if the state had posted a "No Loving Allowed" sign on their bedroom door.

Virginia's law against interracial marriage turned the Lovings' marital bliss into a clandestine operation. The young couple was dragged to court simply for saying "I do" to each other. At their trial, a judge actually dared to declare that God Almighty put different races on separate continents for a reason – apparently God moonlights as a segregationist travel agent in this judge's mind. It's the kind of logic that makes you tilt your head like a confused puppy. The judge basically said mixing races was against divine intent, as if the heavens were up there facepalming at the sight of Richard and Mildred sharing a slice of wedding cake. One can only imagine God listening to that court ruling and going, "I said what about continents now? Don't drag me into this, your Honor." The Lovings (yes, that's really their last name – you can't make this stuff up) were found guilty of... loving. Their sentence? Leave Virginia and don't come back for 25 years, or go to jail. Essentially, they were banished from their home state for the high crime of marriage. If irony could fuel a car, Richard and Mildred would have zoomed off into the sunset with a full tank.

Exiled from Virginia, the couple set up life in the slightly more enlightenment-friendly Washington D.C., but they missed home. They were like Romeo and Juliet if those star-crossed lovers had actually survived and gotten a crappy apartment together across state lines. Mildred eventually got fed up and wrote a letter to Attorney General Bobby Kennedy (because why not shoot for the stars when your own state is being ridiculous?). To their surprise, that letter was forwarded to the ACLU, and soon the Lovings had serious legal firepower on their side. Cue the montage of lawyers in 1960s skinny ties flipping through law books, determined to right this cosmic wrong. Fast forward to 1967: flower power is in the air, Thurgood Marshall is dropping truth bombs on segregation, and the Supreme Court of the United States is about to have its say in *Loving v. Virginia*. The case's name alone sounded like a fairytale showdown – Love versus Virginia, with marriage as the ultimate prize.

In a unanimous decision (because who'd want to be the one justice saying "actually, maybe love shouldn't win" and forever be known as the anti-cupid?), the Supreme Court struck down those Jim Crow-era marriage laws. Chief Justice Earl Warren basically said, "Enough of this nonsense, love is love, y'all." Okay, not in those exact words, but close enough. At long last, Richard and Mildred could stroll through Virginia without fear of handcuffs, perhaps even hold hands in public and scandalize a few old busybodies for good measure. Better yet, couples of all racial combos across America suddenly had the constitutional green light to put a ring on it. Virginia had to retire its unofficial post-Civil War dating rulebook. "Virginia is for Lovers," the state would famously advertise years later – and they finally meant *all* lovers, not just the monochromatic kind.

Marriage Lesson: Love conquers law when the law is wrong. The Lovings taught the world that marriage isn't a privilege for some groups – it's a right for all. In the face of absurd prejudice dressed up as legislation, their story proves that sometimes the most revolutionary act is simply loving who you love, openly and without apology. Love, as it turns out, won't be policed, and even the Supreme Court can't resist a good love story with a happy ending.

An Apartheid Love Story

Travel back a few decades earlier to the late 1940s, and hop continents over to southern Africa and London – yes, simultaneously. This tale has all the makings of a blockbuster romance: a dashing African prince (actual royalty, no less), a charming Englishwoman, and enough political intrigue to make *The Crown* look like a sedate tea party. Our leading man is Seretse Khama, heir to the throne of a tribe in Bechuanaland (today's Botswana). Picture a young prince sent to London for school. Instead of returning with just a degree and some snazzy British suits, Seretse comes back with a bride named Ruth

Williams – a white British woman he fell head over heels for at a social dance. In a Hollywood rom-com, this is where everyone would cheer. In 1948, however, half the planet seemingly lost its mind over this interracial, international love match.

When Seretse and Ruth's marriage came to light, it sparked a geopolitical melodrama. The British Empire (still clinging to its last shreds of colonial pomp) promptly had a royal conniption. Officials labeled it "The Unfortunate Marriage," as if the prince had married a horse or something, rather than, you know, a fellow human being who just happened not to match his skin tone. Back in Seretse's homeland, his uncle – the acting chief – blew a gasket too, forbidding the marriage. Tribal elders were initially horrified that their future leader married a white woman without their blessing. It was basically *Guess Who's Coming to Dinner* on steroids, with colonial officials, tribal politics, and even the racist government of apartheid South Africa all grabbing popcorn to watch the drama.

The lovebirds, however, were unbowed. Seretse and Ruth tied the knot in a simple registry office when even the local church got cold feet about mixing holy water with interracial vows. That's right, they couldn't find a church willing to marry them because the British government leaned on the clergy – divine love had to yield to the Empire's racial neuroses, apparently. So the couple said "I do" in a quick civil ceremony, probably with a clerk who shrugged and thought all the fuss was absurd. But this was real life, and the British authorities promptly exiled the newlyweds as if they were a dangerous contagion. They barred Seretse from returning to his own homeland unless he ditched his wife. Essentially, "Come home without that woman or don't come home at all" – a choice straight out of a twisted fairy tale where the king's advisors are the villains.

For years, Seretse and Ruth lived in limbo in England's dreary embrace, while back in Bechuanaland an empty throne collected dust. Meanwhile, South Africa's apartheid regime practically lost its mind at the mere thought of an African leader with a white wife next door. They pressured Britain to keep Seretse sidelined, and Britain, hoping to appease its racist allies, obliged by extending his exile. It was a true test of love – could it survive being ground up in the gears of global politics?

But true love, being the stubborn force it is, persevered. Ruth and Seretse started a family, and their bond only strengthened under pressure. Their determination paid off: by the mid-1950s, the British finally caved. A new government allowed Seretse and Ruth to return to Africa. Seretse even renounced his claim to the chieftainship as a concession for the homecoming. It's not every day you see a prince give up a crown for love, but hey, anything for a happily ever after. Once back home, Seretse jumped into politics, and within a decade he led Bechuanaland to independence as the new nation of Botswana. Then he became its first president – with Ruth as the First Lady, no less. Talk about a comeback: that "unfortunate" marriage the naysayers griped about ended up forging one of Africa's most stable democracies. Imagine the stiff British officials from earlier, choking on their tea as Seretse and Ruth proudly stood at Botswana's helm.

Marriage Lesson: Love can be mightier than kingdoms and color lines. Seretse and Ruth proved that sometimes you have to fight the world for your love – and that fight can literally change a nation. When society, family, or even empires stand in the way, a united couple can stand taller. Their story teaches that true love doesn't just accept differences – it triumphs over those who refuse to accept them.

The Minnesota Two: Loophole Wedding of 1971

Now let's slide over to Middle America in the groovy early 1970s – a time of bell-bottoms, disco balls, and, apparently, some incredibly creative law-hacking by love-struck individuals. Meet Jack Baker and Michael McConnell, two Minneapolis men who did something in 1971 that was as unthinkable to most folks as a silent disco in a library. They got married. Yes, two grooms, one marriage license, at a time when even suggesting such a thing made most courthouse clerks do a cartoonish double take. But Jack and Michael were determined and, dare we say, a bit mischievous. If their love story were a heist movie, this was the part where they plot to beat the system – except the vault was the Minnesota marriage law, and the tools were more paper and ink than explosives.

The pair first tried the straightforward approach: they walked into a county office and applied for a marriage license like any ordinary couple. The clerk likely blinked and stammered, "You fellas must be joking," before denying them outright. A lesser duo might have slunk away, but not these two. Jack, a law student with a twinkle in his eye, saw a puzzle to solve. If the law didn't explicitly say "no," maybe there was a way to get a "yes." So he hatched a cheeky plan: Jack legally changed his name to the gender-neutral "Pat Lyn." With a new ID for one Pat Lyn McConnell (taking Michael's last name too for good measure), the duo slipped over to a different county where they were unknown. It was the perfect con – and their only loot was a marriage certificate.

This time, when Pat Lyn and Michael applied for a license in Blue Earth County, the paperwork looked ordinary enough to slide under the radar. The clerk either didn't notice anything unusual or just didn't ask questions. License granted! With that precious document in hand, Jack and Michael exchanged vows on a quiet September day in 1971, officiated by a friendly minister who figured love is love. They became, as far as anyone can tell, the first same-sex married couple in U.S. history. No parade, no hashtag campaign – just two men saying "I do" to each other, sealing it with a kiss and a wry smile.

When news of their "loophole wedding" eventually trickled out, the media had a minor frenzy. Society in 1971 just wasn't ready for this kind of matrimony. People freaked out, with some predicting the end of civilization as we know it. You know, the old "what's next, people marrying their goldfish?" slippery-slope routine – because whenever love breaks a norm, someone always insists the sky is falling. The authorities were flustered too. Minnesota officials scrambled to invalidate the union – essentially saying, "Nope, that wedding never happened, no way, not on our watch." The case bounced through the courts until the Minnesota Supreme Court finally ruled that marriage was, in their view, strictly a boy-girl thing. Jack and Michael's legal victory was snatched away. It was a setback, as if the law itself wagged a finger and said, "Nice try, fellas, but not so fast."

Yet despite the official smackdown, Jack and Michael never backed down or split up. They kept that marriage certificate tucked in their files and carried on as a married couple, letting the world slowly catch up. It took until 2015 – a full 44 years later – for the U.S. Supreme Court to catch the vibe and legalize same-sex marriage nationwide. By then Jack and Michael were older gentlemen, likely amused that the rest of America finally showed up to the party they quietly started back in '71.

Marriage Lesson: Sometimes love has to break a few rules (or cleverly bend them) to make history. Jack and Michael taught us that progress often starts with ordinary people daring to live as if the world were already the way it should be. Their crafty, quiet rebellion whispers a truth that eventually grew loud and clear: love is love, and given time (and maybe a clever loophole), it will win. The path to marriage equality was long and winding, but these two proved that even in the unlikeliest of times, change begins with a couple of brave souls and an unshakable bond.

May-December Mischief

Finally, let's rewind to the 1950s for a tale that's less about love conquering barriers and more about, well, pushing wildly inappropriate boundaries. If the other stories in this chapter warm your heart, this one is more like a rock 'n' roll soap opera that makes you cringe as much as laugh. Enter Jerry Lee Lewis: a piano-thumping wild man of early rock, famous for setting pianos (and charts) on fire with hits like "Great Balls of Fire." Jerry was the kind of guy who looked at Elvis Presley's tame hip-shaking and said, "Hold my beer." But in 1958, Jerry did something that put his career in a nosedive and made him the poster boy for why we have marriage laws. He married his 13-year-old cousin. Yes, you read that right: thirteen, as in barely a teenager, and cousin, as in family. Cue the collective "Ew!" heard 'round the world.

Jerry Lee Lewis was 22 at the time – old enough to know better, you'd think. His bride, Myra Gale Brown, wasn't even old enough to attend a high school dance without a chaperone. To add an extra dash of yikes, Myra was Jerry's first cousin once removed (in plain terms, still his cousin, because any way you slice it, marrying your own kin is not okay). This was the 1950s, a supposedly wholesome era of sock hops and malt shops, yet here was a famous rocker basically speed-running the "cancel yourself" challenge decades before Twitter could do it for him. When the news broke – during a tour in England, no less – the press and public reacted with a unified disgust usually reserved for finding a rat in your soda. Reporters bluntly asked, "Who is that girl you're calling your wife?" When Jerry answered honestly, jaws hit the floor. He even tried to claim she was 15 instead of 13 at first, as if that made it any better – which tells you he knew it was wrong, too.

The backlash was swift and brutal. Jerry Lee went from rock 'n' roll royalty to radioactive overnight. Concerts were canceled, radio stations refused to play his records, and he was effectively blacklisted from the industry for a time. Turns out even the freewheeling '50s had their limits, and marrying a child (who also happens to be your cousin) was beyond those limits. Who knew? (Everyone. Literally everyone knew, Jerry.) In the American South back then, a 13-year-old could actually marry with parental permission – believe it or not. So legally, Jerry's wedding wasn't null and void. But socially and morally, it was about as welcome as a skunk at a garden party. The scandal put a spotlight on how disturbingly lax child marriage laws were in the U.S., and people started clamoring for change.

In the years that followed, states slowly began raising minimum marriage ages and closing the loopholes that had allowed such extreme May-December unions. It's not like Congress rushed through a "Jerry Lee Lewis Act" the day after, but his debacle became the cautionary tale lawmakers would bring up when pushing for reform. "Remember that rock star?" they'd whisper, while shaking their heads. Meanwhile, Jerry Lee's personal life kept unraveling like a country song played in reverse. The marriage to Myra eventually fell apart – surprise, a middle schooler and a twenty-something rockstar were not a recipe for happily ever after. Myra grew up (as she was bound to do) and wised up. Jerry's career did recover some in later years (America has a weird habit of forgiving celebrities), but his reputation never fully shook off the ick of that scandal.

Marriage Lesson: Sometimes "love" (or what someone claims is love) needs boundaries – like, say, don't marry someone who needs permission to stay up past 10 PM. Society learned from Jerry Lee Lewis's misadventure that age gaps can be more than just numbers; they can be chasms of maturity and power that no amount of rock 'n' roll swagger can bridge. The takeaway? Love may be crazy, but it isn't supposed to be *that* crazy. True love uplifts and inspires – it doesn't require calling the cops or a PR crisis team. In other words, if your marriage announcement doubles as a scandal, you probably did something very wrong.

Chapter 8

Love in the Late 20th – From Taboo to Turning Point

Apartheid's Final Frontier: South Africa's Repeal of Mixed-Race Marriage Bans (1985)

Picture South Africa in the early 1980s: pop songs are blaring on the radio, neon fashion is in, and the apartheid government is acting like the ultimate overbearing parent. And I do mean overbearing – these guys had rules about who you could love or marry based purely on skin color. Seriously. Back in 1949 they passed a law that basically said, "No, you absolutely may not fall in love with that person if their melanin doesn't match yours." It was officially the Prohibition of Mixed Marriages Act, but it might as well have been the No Swirling Allowed rule. The regime drew a bold line through Cupid's playground: whites on one side, everyone else on the other. If Cupid dared cross that line, he'd get a nasty citation from the love police.

To enforce this love embargo, apartheid officials went to absurd lengths. There were actual "morality police" who would raid homes and arrest couples for the *crime* of being in an interracial relationship. (Imagine officers barging in, holding up paint swatches to compare skin tones—yes, it was as creepy and ridiculous as it sounds.) Yet, despite the risk of jail or worse, many brave couples still found ways to be together. Some snuck out of the country to marry abroad where apartheid's rules couldn't reach. They'd elope to places like Swaziland, say "I do" where it was legal, then sneak back and live as if they were just roommates. It was the romantic equivalent of bootlegging: forbidden but impossible to resist.

One famous story is Sandra Laing, who basically broke apartheid's brain by just existing. Born to white parents but looking Black, Sandra was a living, breathing glitch in the racist matrix. Her very identity threw the system into chaos. Fast forward to her teenage years: she falls in love with a Black man named Petrus. By 16, Sandra said "to heck with these laws" and ran off to marry him. Because they couldn't legally wed in South Africa, they eloped across the border. Her father went ballistic – legend has it he threatened to shoot her *and* himself if she ever came home. Apartheid officials were no kinder: to live with her husband and kids openly, Sandra had to pull off the absurd feat of changing her official race classification. (If the government says you're white, your own non-white kids could be taken away from you. Yes, really.) Imagine having to petition the state to *change your race* just to keep your family together – that's how deranged these laws were.

Sandra's saga had star-crossed love, family drama, and bureaucratic insanity. And she wasn't alone. Plenty of interracial couples risked everything to be together. Each stolen kiss across color lines was a tiny act of rebellion. Some couples pretended to be maid and master in their own homes to avoid suspicion – a charade worthy of a telenovela, but it beat getting thrown in jail. Through the 70s and 80s, these lovers quietly kept the flame alive while apartheid tried to douse it with legal cold water.

By the mid-1980s, it was clear even to the apartheid regime that this was a losing battle. You can patrol a border, but you can't patrol hearts. Facing growing internal protests and global side-eye from the rest of the world, South Africa's rulers decided to make a token concession. In 1985, with zero fanfare, they *repealed* the ban on mixed marriages. Just like that, decades of "forbidden love" restrictions went poof. One day it was a crime for a white and a Black South African to tie the knot; the next day, totally fine. No apology, no big speeches – the officials basically shrugged and quietly moved on, probably hoping nobody would make a big deal of it.

Of course, for the couples involved, it was a huge deal. At long last, they could get legally married at home without risking prison or exile. I bet the first interracial pair to walk into a South African marriage office in '85 kept waiting for someone to yell "Psych! Just kidding!" But it was real. The law finally stepped out of the way of love, at least in that regard. This was one of apartheid's final frontiers crumbling. Though the whole evil system didn't collapse until a decade later, love managed to score a major victory.

Marriage Lesson: No matter how hard they try, lawmakers can't legislate away love. Apartheid's ban on mixed marriages was doomed to fail because people will love who they love, period. Eventually, even the most stubborn government had to face reality: the human heart was way more powerful than their ridiculous rule book. Love's stubborn defiance pushed the law to catch up – a lesson that echoes far beyond South Africa.

The Rainbow Revolution Begins: Denmark's 1989 Same-Sex Partnership Pioneers

Now let's hop over to Europe in the late 1980s. Big hair and synth-pop are all the rage, and a radical new idea is floating in the air: maybe, just maybe, two people of the same sex should be able to say "I do" (or at least "I officially commit"). Denmark, 1989 – not exactly where most of the world expected a marriage revolution, but that's where one quietly began. While many countries were still stuck in "don't ask, don't tell" mode, the Danes basically said, "Hold our beer – we've got a new kind of wedding to plan."

In 1989, Denmark became the first country on planet Earth to legally recognize same-sex partnerships. They called it a "registered partnership" because the word *marriage* was a bit too spicy for some tastes. But make no mistake: it was essentially marriage with an asterisk. This was bold. It was *fabulous*. And it went down at Copenhagen City Hall with a deputy mayor officiating like it was the most normal thing ever.

The poster boys of this rainbow milestone were Axel and Eigil Axgil, a pair of older gents who had been together for 40 years (practically a lifetime, gay or straight!). On October 1, 1989, dressed in matching suits, these two said "Ja!" and became the first same-sex couple in the world to be legally wed-ish. They even shared a last name, "Axgil" – a combo of their first names – which is about as cute as it gets. Outside City Hall, reporters gathered as if it were a royal wedding. Axel and Eigil sealed the deal with a kiss in a horse-drawn carriage, champagne in hand. The crowd cheered, cameras flashed, and a few conservative onlookers probably gasped into their coffee.

But Denmark didn't crumble, society survived, and the only thing falling from the sky was confetti, not fire and brimstone.

Denmark's big move lit a small spark that would eventually catch on elsewhere. Think of it as the pilot episode of *Marriage Equality: The Series*. At first, some places gave it a standing ovation, others hurriedly changed the channel. But the seed was planted. Suddenly, the idea of legally recognized same-sex couples wasn't hypothetical; it was on the news, with two smiling grooms cutting a wedding cake and everything. In 1989, pop culture wasn't exactly brimming with gay weddings – Ellen was still in the closet and *Will & Grace* hadn't even aired – so this real-life event was huge. It's like society's software got a surprise update and everyone had to deal with the new terms and conditions.

Not everyone was on board, of course. Plenty of politicians elsewhere predicted that civilization would fall apart if gay couples got legal status. You know, the usual sky-is-falling routine. But Denmark's example quietly put those fears to shame. It's hard to argue "the world will end!" when boring old Monday morning comes and nothing's changed except a few couples got a legal piece of paper and some tax benefits.

Leave it to the famously sensible, cozy Danes to make a social revolution feel as comfy as sitting by the fireplace. They didn't throw a giant parade that day (though Pride parades would flourish soon enough), but they did something enduring: they proved that the law can treat love between any two adults with respect and the world keeps spinning. The phrase "love is love" wasn't a cliché yet – Denmark basically helped coin it by example.

The ripple effect of that day in Copenhagen would take time to spread. But spread it did. In the following years, a few neighbors (hello, Norway and Sweden) tiptoed into the partnership pool. By the turn of the century, the Netherlands said "heck, let's call it marriage and be done with it," becoming the first to fully legalize same-sex marriage in 2001. One by one, countries followed like a slow but steady falling row of dominoes. It all traces back to that Danish beginning. In '89, Denmark was a lone pioneer, a tiny country sending up a flare that love deserved equal rights. It would take a while, but the world was watching – and eventually, even the slowpokes and naysayers had to admit this whole equality thing wasn't going away.

Marriage Lesson: Sometimes the heart sprints ahead and the law has to hustle to catch up. Denmark's little rainbow revolution showed that progress often starts quietly, with one brave step. Love refused to stay invisible, and in at least one happy corner of the world, the law opened its eyes. It was the beginning of a global lesson that would echo for years: you can't hold back love's tide forever without looking absolutely ridiculous.

From Hawaii with Love (and Lawsuits): The 1990s Marriage Showdown

Cue the tropical music: it's the early 1990s in Hawaii, a place synonymous with romance. People fly there for honeymoons and sunset weddings. But in 1993, Hawaii became ground zero for a marriage earthquake no one saw coming. Three same-sex couples walked into Honolulu's marriage license office and said, "Aloha, we'd like a license please." It sounds like the setup to a joke, but what followed was more like a high-stakes courtroom drama.

When those couples were (predictably) denied, they didn't shrug and hit the beach – they sued the state in a case called Baehr v. Lewin. And shocker: the Hawaii Supreme Court actually took them seriously. In 1993, the court hinted that denying same-sex couples the right to marry might violate the state's constitution. In plain English: unless the state had a really solid reason to say "no," it would have to start saying "yes." *Huge* news. Suddenly, it looked like Hawaii might become the Las Vegas of gay weddings. Couples all over America were daydreaming about flying to Waikiki to tie the knot and then bringing that shiny Hawaiian marriage certificate back home.

That's when a lot of folks in power absolutely lost their cool. Picture conservative lawmakers in D.C. sweating through their suits at the thought of two grooms from Honolulu showing up in Kansas demanding recognition as a married couple. The political panic button was slapped hard. Opponents trotted out the classic slippery slope arguments – "if we let Adam marry Steve today, someone will want to marry their goldfish tomorrow!" (Newsflash: no one married a goldfish. The republic survived.) Congress hastily passed the Defense of Marriage Act (DOMA) in 1996. It was billed like a heroic measure to "save" marriage – as if love needed rescuing from these pesky couples. In reality, DOMA basically said: federally, marriage means one man and one woman, and no state has to honor any "untraditional" marriages from elsewhere. It was a preemptive strike, aimed squarely at Hawaii's potential rainbow revolution. And fun fact: President Bill Clinton, of all people, signed it into law (yes, the same Bill who would later be known for a scandal or two about the sanctity of his *own* marriage – oh the irony).

Meanwhile in Hawaii, the legal saga continued. In 1996, a trial court actually ruled in favor of the couples – theoretically clearing the way for same-sex marriages to start. But before any could happen, Hawaii's voters stepped in and passed a constitutional amendment in 1998 to block it. It was like Hawaii told those couples, "We love you, but we're not ready to commit." Cue sad violins. No marriage licenses were issued after all; the party was over before it began.

In the short term, same-sex marriage in the U.S. was shoved back into the closet, legally speaking. DOMA slammed the federal door shut, and dozens of states enacted their own mini-DOMAs just to be extra sure. It was like a nationwide "not so fast!" to the idea of gay weddings. But something was different now: the topic was out in the open. What had been unthinkable was suddenly a matter of public debate. The genie was out of the bottle, and it wasn't going back in. By the way, about twenty years later, the White House would be lit up with rainbow lights to celebrate nationwide marriage equality – but back in the '90s, that outcome felt like pure fantasy. Even pop culture picked up on the shift. In 1996, *Friends* featured a lesbian wedding (Ross's ex-wife marries her partner), and it made waves – some TV stations refused to air it, but many viewers saw it and thought "neat, a wedding with two brides." By 1998, *Will & Grace* was on primetime, bringing gay characters (albeit single ones) into America's living rooms. The idea of same-sex couples building a life together was inching its way from controversy toward normalcy.

Marriage Lesson: Love can be delayed, but it can't be denied. Hawaii's almost-wedding bells sent a message that echoed beyond its shores: even when lawmakers build walls and pass bans, love keeps pushing at the boundaries. The heart doesn't quit just because it's told "no." In the end, all those setbacks only underscored the point – love's stubborn defiance will eventually make the law come around. It might take time, but spoiler alert: love wins.

Love Without Borders: 1990s Cross-Cultural Cupid and International Knot-Tying

As the 1990s rolled on, the world was getting smaller – not just via the internet and global TV, but in the realm of romance too. The Cold War thawed, travel opened up, and people started falling head over heels across borders and cultures like never before. Love had frequent-flyer miles and wasn't afraid to use them. The result? A boom in cross-cultural and international marriages that forced governments to play catch-up.

Suddenly, a typical love story might be: boy meets girl *from a different continent.* Or childhood pen pals from opposite sides of the world realize, "Uh-oh, I think we're in love." U.S. servicemen stationed abroad, foreign students at colleges, backpackers finding romance on the road – the scenarios were endless. The 90s teemed with these Cupid-gone-global tales. Embassies and immigration offices quickly found themselves swimming in international wedding paperwork.

Enter the unsung hero of many an international love story: the K-1 fiancé visa (cue the *90 Day Fiancé* theme song). This U.S. visa became so popular it inspired a reality TV show years later, but back then it was simply the golden ticket for your foreign sweetheart to come get married. The catch? Once they arrive, you've got 90 days to walk down the aisle or they walk back onto a plane. Talk about deadline pressure! It's the stuff of rom-coms – will the couple overcome culture shock, disapproving relatives, and cold feet in time?

Many did, sometimes with hilarious misunderstandings along the way.

Then there was the rise of the so-called mail-order bride industry. The term alone raised eyebrows. Basically, matchmaking agencies connected Western singles with potential spouses in far-off lands. It had a whiff of transactional ickiness, but by the 90s it had gone semi-mainstream – everyone seemed to know a story about someone who tried it. Some of those stories were sweet (real love in an unexpected place), others were total cautionary tales. Let's just say results varied – some couples truly fell in love and thrived, and others… not so much.

With love crossing continents, governments faced a tangle of conflicting marriage laws. Maybe a marriage was perfectly legal in one country but not recognized in another because of different age limits or divorce rules. Perhaps someone had a spouse in a country where polygamy was allowed (yikes). The lawyers got a workout untangling who was actually married to whom, and where. It was like a soap opera written in legal code.

On the cultural side, international couples sometimes encountered raised eyebrows or outright prejudice. A Western guy with an Asian bride might hear snide "mail-order" remarks even if they met naturally. A mixed-race or cross-cultural pair might get stares in homogenous hometowns. But mostly, these couples were busy learning each other's languages, cuisines, and holiday traditions – proving that love can be a pretty great cultural exchange program. Sure, there were bumps along the way (misunderstandings, in-law culture clashes, debates over which holidays to celebrate), but many families discovered that having in-laws from another country was actually kind of cool. Double the holidays, double the food!

All this global romance did prompt some new rules. After a few horror stories (say, a supposedly "perfect" foreign husband turned out to be a creep), the U.S. and others started regulating international matchmakers and beefing up visa vetting. Background checks, interviews about "how did you meet" and "what's your spouse's favorite food" – governments basically became part-time love detectives. Awkward for genuine couples, but it helped weed out a few bad actors.

In the end, the 1990s set the stage for a world where love truly became borderless. Those cross-cultural couples helped make the world feel a bit smaller and more connected. Neighbors got introduced to new cultures through wedding ceremonies and potluck dinners. Skeptics learned that, surprise, people from different backgrounds can actually be soulmates. And lawmakers, after initially scrambling, gradually adjusted policies to reality – because love wasn't going to fill out forms in triplicate for permission.

Marriage Lesson: Love knows no borders – and it will gleefully leap over any wall while the law scrambles behind with a passport and paperwork. In the 1990s, global love laughed at distance and red tape, forcing governments to adapt or be left in the dust. The heart doesn't care about nationality or culture; it just finds its match and goes for it. And sooner or later, even the stodgiest officials had to admit that when love goes global, the laws had better keep up with the heart's stubborn, world-traveling defiance.

Chapter 9

Modern Love – New Millennium, New Milestones (2000s–2020s)

Marriage Equality Mania

Picture this: It's April 1, 2001, just after midnight, and the city of Amsterdam is throwing a party that would make Cupid proud. Four couples line up at City Hall – but these aren't your grandma's weddings. We've got grooms marrying grooms and brides marrying brides, and the Mayor is presiding with a smile wider than a wedding cake. This is marriage equality mania kicking off, and no, it's not an April Fool's joke. The Netherlands becomes the first country to shout, "Love is love – now in legal flavor!" The world tilted on its axis ever so slightly to make room for a dance floor big enough for everyone.

Soon enough, other countries join the conga line. One by one, nations across Europe and beyond start saying "I do" to same-sex marriage. Canada and Spain cut in around 2005, South Africa tosses confetti in 2006, and by the mid-2010s more than two dozen countries had opened their wedding chapels to LGBTQ+ couples. It's like a bunch of dominoes in veils falling – toppling the old notion that marriage was an exclusive club for one man and one woman only. The new millennium decided marriage should be the hottest party in town and everyone's invited.

In the United States, the road to the altar was a bit like a dramatic TV series – *Will & Grace* meets courtroom thriller. Massachusetts eloped with equality in 2004, becoming the cool kid on the block, while other states fought it out in court or at the ballot box with all the drama of a soap opera. There were plot twists (looking at you, California – legalizing, then un-legalizing, then legalizing again). By the time the issue reached the U.S. Supreme Court, it felt like the season finale. And love won big. In June 2015, Obergefell v. Hodges essentially RSVP'd "yes" to every same-sex couple's wedding across all 50 states. Cue the nationwide jubilee: the White House lit up in rainbow colors, people danced in the streets, and champagne corks popped from coast to coast. The Supreme Court Justices probably didn't picture themselves as grand marshals of a pride parade, but there they were, on a parade float of legalese and glitter.

Weddings themselves got a fabulous upgrade. Marriage equality meant double the brides, double the grooms, and a whole lot of reinvented traditions. Who leads the first dance? Whichever partner has the better moves. Two bouquets to toss? Sure – double the chance for eager singles to catch one. Some ceremonies ditched "Here Comes the Bride" for Lady Gaga anthems, and wedding hashtags went from the mundane to gems like #TwoBridesBetterThanOne. What used to be radical became remarkably routine – and with better dance playlists.

Of course, progress came with a side of *cake wars*. Yes, we need to talk about the baker who refused to bake that cake. A few flustered bakeries in the 2010s wouldn't make wedding cakes for gay couples, apparently worried that two little grooms on a cake topper would make their oven explode. One case even reached the Supreme Court

– essentially a showdown of *cake rights vs. wrongs*. The absurdity was not lost on anyone: "Let them eat cake" took on new meaning. Meanwhile, countless other bakers happily piped rainbows on cakes for whoever asked, because love (and business) is sweet. It turned out equality tasted like multi-layered vanilla sponge with rainbow frosting.

By the late 2010s, marriage equality had gone from *controversial* to *commonplace*. The sight of two brides walking down the aisle was as unremarkable as an overly enthusiastic DJ doing the Chicken Dance at a reception. Sure, a few grumblers lingered – that one uncle stuck in 1950, a politician muttering about slippery slopes – but the sky didn't fall. In fact, one kid in 2020 reportedly asked his mom, "Can boys marry boys?" When told yes, he just shrugged and said, "Cool. Can I have a cookie?" That's normalization in a nutshell.

Marriage Equality Mania taught us a lesson as sweet as buttercream: love wins, eventually. Society's understanding of matrimony stretched to include everyone, and the institution didn't collapse – it threw a bigger party. By expanding marriage to same-sex couples, we didn't ruin it; we revitalized it. The law had to scramble to keep up with love, and when it finally did, the world collectively said, "About time! Now where's the open bar?" Modern love proved that when it comes to who can marry whom, the heart knows best – and the law will follow, one fabulous wedding at a time.

No Kidding – Ending Child Marriage

Let's switch gears from adults acting like lovestruck teens to actual teens (and sometimes actual children) being wed off as if puberty were the new twenty-one. Sounds crazy, right? Yet in the early 2000s, the world got a harsh reality check: child marriage wasn't just something from a dusty Victorian novel or an episode of *Game of Thrones* – it was still happening, sometimes shockingly close to home. It turned out some laws had more loopholes than a crochet sweater. Sure, on paper it was "18 and up" to marry, but then came the fine print: exceptions if a judge approved, if parents signed off, or – wildest of all – if the girl was pregnant (because someone thought, "She's having a baby, so why not throw a husband in the mix? What could possibly go wrong?"). The result? Stories straight out of a nightmare: middle-school-aged girls walking down aisles they had no business being on.

Enter the heroes who said, "Not on our watch." Across the globe and in local communities, campaigns revved up to slam those loopholes shut and raise the marriage age to a non-creepy level (ahem, 18). In Tanzania, a young activist named Rebeca Gyumi basically hauled the old marriage law into court in 2016 and drop-kicked it. The law had allowed girls as young as 14 to marry (while boys had to be 18 – talk about a gross double standard). Rebeca argued this was unconstitutional and flat-out wrong, and the judges agreed. Boom – Tanzania raised the age to 18 for everyone, sending a clear message that school uniforms and wedding veils should not overlap.

Over in the U.S., a survivor named Sherry Johnson turned her personal tragedy into a crusade. She had been forced to marry at age 11 (yes, eleven – an age when most of us were worrying about math homework, not marriage vows). In her case, the adults around her thought the "solution" to her being pregnant (after a rape, no less) was to marry her off to the 20-something-year-old perpetrator. Florida's laws at the time basically shrugged and said "sure, why not." Sherry spent years pushing Florida lawmakers to see the insanity of this. By

2018, largely thanks to her, Florida raised its marriage minimum and trimmed down those outrageous exceptions. It wasn't a perfect fix (they still allowed 17 with conditions), but it was progress. And Sherry's activism lit a fire under other states to check their own rules and say, "Wait, are we okay with child brides? Let's not be."

Meanwhile, the movement to end child marriage was going full throttle worldwide. Countries from Malawi to India toughened up their laws, often prodded by activists and former child brides who'd had enough. The slogan "Girls Not Brides" became a global rallying cry. Street plays in village squares, billboards, and social media campaigns all hammered home the point that kids belong in school, not in wedding halls. Celebrities chimed in too – imagine a famous comedian joking on late-night TV, "If you're not old enough to vote for your future, you probably shouldn't be marrying your future spouse!" Public outrage grew every time a story went viral about a ten-year-old in a wedding dress, and legislators, feeling the heat, started closing the loopholes faster than you can say "I object."

By the 2020s, the tide was turning. Many places set 18 as the hard minimum age for marriage, no exceptions, finally aligning the law with common sense. Sure, a few regions lagged behind or clung to archaic exceptions (there's always someone late to the party), but the momentum was clear. Childhood was being reclaimed from the clutches of premature matrimony. The lesson in this "No Kidding" saga? Marriage is for grown-ups – period. Modern love isn't just about expanding who can marry, but making sure those walking down the aisle are actually ready for the journey. By kicking kiddie weddings to the curb, society reminded itself that protecting childhood isn't just about keeping kids in school and play – it's also about saving the institution of marriage from scenarios that belong in horror films. After all, there's plenty of time to say "I do" – no need to rush into lifelong vows before you're even old enough to drive.

Three's (Not) a Crowd?

If you thought two people trying to navigate marriage was tricky, some folks in the new millennium said, "Why not add more?" Polyamory – loving more than one person with everyone's blessing – stepped into the spotlight and right up to the altar (well, sort of). For centuries, monogamy was the only setting (no expansion pack available), but now some folks were beta-testing the multiplayer mode. For the longest time, marriage law was a strict two-player game. Sure, old-school polygamy existed (one guy, multiple wives, usually looking like a reality show with too few bathrooms), but modern polyamory is a different animal: all genders, all partners considered equal, and *consent, consent, consent.* As the 2000s and 2010s rolled on, enough people were in multi-partner relationships that the law began hearing some unusual requests: "Hey, can we get legal recognition for our trio? Pretty please?"

In 2020, Somerville, Massachusetts became the first city in the U.S. to officially say, "Yeah, we can work with that." The city council, likely unfazed by just about anything, created a domestic partnership ordinance that let more than two consenting adults register as a family. Suddenly, throuples (and quartets) in Somerville could visit each other in the hospital, share health benefits, and generally feel validated that their love wasn't totally invisible to the powers that be. Not to be outdone, a public notary in Brazil had already made waves in the 2010s by recognizing a three-person union (in one case, three women!). It wasn't "marriage" in the traditional sense – Brazilian law didn't have a form for that – but it was a legal acknowledgment that love isn't always binary. These trailblazing cases were like beta tests for multi-partner matrimony, and they got everyone from lawyers to late-night comedians talking.

Of course, adding extra people to a marriage makes everything hilariously complicated. The law books weren't written for "spouse #3" fields. Imagine the paperwork for a three-way divorce, or the courtroom drama of four parents fighting for custody of two kids and a parrot. Tax filing as a thruple? Good luck, accountants. It's the kind of legal spaghetti that gives bureaucrats headaches and keeps philosophers musing, "Is there a limit to how many people can share love – or a mortgage?"

Socially, these multi-partner unions pushed a lot of buttons. Skeptics squawked about the end of the traditional family and trotted out the slippery slope ("What's next, marrying your houseplant?" to which polyamorists groaned, "We're humans in love, not botany enthusiasts, thanks"). The people in these relationships countered that they were literally building bigger families out of love – how's that a bad thing? Media took interest, featuring polyamorous families in documentaries and reality TV. Viewers saw that a household with three or four adults was not some wild orgy 24/7; more often it was about whose turn it was to cook dinner or which two were going to chaperone the kids' field trip. And sure, there might be three mothers-in-law to juggle at Thanksgiving, but poly folks handle it. In other words, mostly ordinary, just with more rings in the jewelry dish. Younger generations mostly shrugged at the idea of throuples; many grew up with the concept of "chosen family" and figured love is love, be it in pairs, triads, or a whole starting lineup.

By the 2020s, only a few places (like Somerville) dared to dip a toe in the legal waters of polyamory, so don't expect Hallmark to roll out a "Happy Anniversary to my three husbands" card line just yet. But the very fact it's being debated and tested is telling. The experiment of multi-partner unions asks society to stretch its definition of marriage once again. The lesson from this polyamorous frontier? Love and commitment aren't one-size-fits-all. Modern love keeps testing boundaries, and even if the legal system is slower than a dial-up modem to catch up, the mere attempt is expanding our collective imagination of what matrimony can be. Two's company, three's a crowd – but maybe, just maybe, three can also be a family. If everyone's happy and in love, why not let them all be part of the same happily-ever-after? Stay tuned, because the story of "happily ever after" might eventually come with an expanded cast.

I Now Pronounce You... Robot and Human?

Just when it seemed marriage couldn't get more expansive, the 21st century came up with, "Hold my bouquet, I'm marrying my (fill in the blank)." We've now seen people "wed" everything from fictional characters to their pet cats. Love truly knows no bounds – or maybe humans are just that quirky.

Consider the case of a Japanese man who literally married a hologram. His bride? A popular virtual singer named Hatsune Miku. He had an actual wedding ceremony in 2019, complete with a white tux and a set of vows. His family did not exactly throw rice at this one (most declined the invite, understandably), but he was happy. Unfortunately, his marital bliss hit a tech snag when the company that made his hologram wife's software discontinued support. One day she's serenading you in the kitchen, next day she's "404 Not Found." Talk about a modern love tragedy – till software update do us part.

Maybe tech romances aren't your thing. How about marrying… yourself? Yes, sologamy became a minor trend. Tired of waiting for Prince or Princess Charming, people (mostly women) started saying "I do" to the one person they can truly count on: themselves. They put on the dress, walk down the aisle solo, recite vows in the mirror about self-love and lifelong commitment to #1. One British woman even took herself on a honeymoon to celebrate. It's equal parts empowering and a bit absurd – a kind of rom-com meets self-care Sunday. And hey, no messy divorce unless you start arguing with your own reflection.

If that's not outlandish enough, some folks decided to forsake fellow humans entirely. We've seen people hold ceremonies to marry their pets – dogs in tiny tuxedos, cats plotting their escape. A British woman married her dog on live TV, saying he was the most loyal partner she'd ever had (the dog, to his credit, didn't object). Then there are the romantics who fall for inanimate objects. A woman in America famously married the Eiffel Tower – yes, the big iron thing in Paris – and even changed her last name to Eiffel. There's a term for this – objectophilia – proving that if you can think of it, someone has probably tried to marry it. These unions aren't legal (you can't get a marriage license for a landmark or a Labrador), but that hasn't stopped people from declaring lifelong devotion in very creative ways.

And let's not forget the beyond-the-grave unions. In France, you can actually marry a dead person under special circumstances. It's called posthumous marriage, and it turns tragedy into a legal love story. Essentially, if your fiancé dies unexpectedly, the French President can approve a marriage that makes you the widow of someone who is, well, already six feet under. It gives a whole new twist to "till death do us part" – more like "till death, then a quick paperwork, do us unite." It's both haunting and heartwarming that love can persist in such a formal way. Not many take this route, but the fact it exists shows that marriage can extend even into the afterlife.

So, what do we learn from all this matrimonial mayhem? For one, the definition of marriage has become as flexible as a yoga instructor. Most of these bizarre marriages aren't legally recognized, but they still make us scratch our heads and reflect. Marriage is clearly more than just a legal status – it's a symbol, a statement, a story we tell about love and commitment (or our quirky sense of humor). Modern love has basically turned the institution of marriage into Play-Doh, molding it into whatever shape suits our desires or imagination. And even if we laugh or roll our eyes at someone marrying a hologram, each example nudges us to ask: why do people marry, and who gets to decide what counts as a "real" marriage?

In the end, the 2000s–2020s showed that matrimony isn't a static concept stuck in a dusty rulebook – it's a living, evolving idea. Love keeps throwing curveballs, and society and the law are left trying to catch them without spilling the champagne. The lesson? Modern love will go wherever it pleases – up to and including the altar – and our definitions of matrimony have to stretch to keep up. It's been a wild ride, and the wedding march isn't over yet. Who knows what or who might be next? One thing's for sure: with love this inventive, "happily ever after" now comes in literally every flavor imaginable.

Chapter 10

Cupid's Legal Laughs – Bizarre Laws and Oddball Facts

Marrying the Dead (Oui, c'est légal!)

Imagine being so in love that not even death can stop your wedding. Sounds like the plot of a Tim Burton movie (hello, *Corpse Bride*), but in France it's real life. Yes, *mon ami*, under French law you can actually marry your deceased sweetheart. It's called posthumous marriage – basically tying the knot with a ghost. You don't get to prop the dearly departed up at the altar *Weekend at Bernie's*-style, but you do get an official marriage certificate with a corpse's name on it. Talk about undying love!

This bizarre legal twist dates back to 1959 and a tragedy that could make a stone cry. A young woman named Irène was engaged to her fiancé when disaster struck – a dam burst (the Malpasset Dam, for history buffs), and he was killed just weeks before the wedding. Heartbroken beyond belief, Irène appealed directly to the French President at the time, General Charles de Gaulle. Picture that scene: a grief-stricken bride pleading, *"Please, let me marry him anyway!"* De Gaulle, probably wiping a tear from his stoic military eye, actually said yes. By the end of that year, the French parliament passed a law allowing posthumous marriage. Leave it to the French to make even "'til death do us part" negotiable.

Of course, you can't just marry a dead person on a whim (no Tinder for ghosts, sorry). The law has fine print. You must prove that, while alive, you two truly intended to marry – as in, wedding date set, invitations sent, or at least a joint Netflix account. You also need the blessing of the departed's family. (In-laws have a say even when your fiancé is six feet under – some things never change.) And the big one: the President of France himself must approve it. Yes, the French President occasionally plays Cupid for ghosts. We imagine this presidential duty comes with its share of *"seriously?"* moments – signing a marriage license for someone who's now a photo on the mantle.

If you clear those hurdles, the wedding goes on – sort of. The marriage is retroactive to the day *before* the person died, which is both romantic and morbidly efficient. Essentially, France says *"Sure, you're married – as long as we pretend he was alive yesterday."* The living spouse gains some emotional closure, but not a payday: you can't claim the dead partner's property or inheritance (no gold-digging the grave, mesdames). And if you were hoping for a fairytale honeymoon, sorry – you'll be honeymooning solo. In fact, a posthumous bride or groom is officially considered a widow/er immediately after "I do." It's a wedding where you start out in sickness and in health, and pretty much skip straight to *"till death"* – since one party is already there.

Believe it or not, hundreds of French citizens have married their late fiancés in the decades since. It's not common, but it's more than just that one tragic dam story. A vast majority of applicants are women, which is revealing in its own way. (Apparently, far more grieving girlfriends yearn to be ghost wives than grieving boyfriends want to be ghost husbands – make of that what you will.) As recently as 2009, a young woman named Magali married her fiancé even after a car accident took his life. She wore black to the ceremony, stood next to a photograph of him, and said "oui" through tears. The local mayor officiated with the power vested in him by the *Code Civil* and, presumably, the Twilight Zone. It was heart-wrenching yet oddly beautiful – a legal seal on love after death.

The cultural impact of this law is profound and a little spooky. France essentially said *love transcends death, and we'll put it in writing*. It's a very French sentiment in a way – dramatic, romantic, and defying conventional rules. Critics might find it absurd ("marrying a ghost, really?"), but to those left behind, it offers closure, honor, even legitimacy (especially if, say, there's a child on the way who can be born to legally married parents). It's the law acting as grief counselor, acknowledging that sometimes our hearts don't move on just because we've lost someone.

Marriage lesson: Sometimes love writes its own rules, and occasionally the law follows. Posthumous marriage, as bizarre as it sounds, is a mirror to the human need for closure and commitment beyond mortality. It shows the lengths society will go to acknowledge love – even when one of the lovers has literally given up the ghost. In its odd way, this law teaches us that marriage isn't just about tax breaks or rings or even living people; it's about our desire to honor a promise. When the law bends to accommodate a broken heart, you see how *human* those dry legal codes can be. Love makes us do crazy things, and here, it made a government say "I do" to a ghost – proving that when it comes to love, sometimes even death isn't the final word.

"I Take Thee, Dare I Do"

We've all done dumb things on a dare – chugging hot sauce, embarrassing dance-offs, questionable haircuts. But how about getting married on a dare? That sounds like a bad college movie plot (or maybe a TikTok challenge gone too far), yet it actually happens often enough that Delaware – otherwise a quiet, tiny U.S. state – decided to address it. In Delaware, if you wake up with a ring on your finger and a vague memory that someone yelled *"I dare you to marry him!"* last night, you're in luck. The law lets you annul that marriage because it was a dare. Essentially, Delaware has a legal "undo" button for marriages that were, in the eyes of the court, one big joke. It's the ultimate morning-after get-out-of-jail-free card.

Picture the scene: a couple of buddies in Vegas, a night of revelry (likely Jägerbombs or whatever the kids drink these days), and one says, *"Bro, you won't marry that girl you just met. Double-dog dare ya!"* Next thing you know, there's an Elvis impersonator officiating and you're saying "I do" while your friends livestream it. Cut to the cold light of day (and a brutal hangover) and you're like, *"We did what?!"* If you happen to hail from Delaware, no worries. You can stroll into court and basically say, *"Uh, we only got married on a dare. We were just kidding."* And the court will literally erase the marriage. It's as if it never happened – like the legal equivalent of annulling a purchase on Amazon because you accidentally clicked "Buy Now."

This isn't urban legend; Delaware's annulment statute explicitly includes marriages that one or both parties entered into "as a jest or dare." You have to love the honesty of that language. Lawmakers basically anticipated the frat-boy antics of the world and said, "Alright, let's make sure these knuckleheads aren't stuck for life because of one stupid stunt." One can only imagine the case that inspired this. Perhaps some influential judge's nephew came home hitched as a prank and Uncle Judge thought, *"Oh heck no, we need a safety net for this nonsense."* Whatever the origin, it's on the books, giving Delaware the prize for the most oddly compassionate marriage law in America.

Here's how it works: you've got to act fast – there's a time limit (you generally need to file for that annulment within 90 days of sobering up, er, discovering the "jest"). The idea is you realized pretty immediately that the marriage was a goof. If you wait a year, you can't exactly say it was just a prank; at that point, buddy, you actually have a spouse. But in that brief window, Delaware courts will drop the curtain on the farce. Only one of you needs to claim you weren't serious. Think about that: your blushing bride *might* have thought it was true love, but if you can prove *you* only did it because of a dare or as a joke, boom – annulled. Kind of harsh, but also a relief for the joker in question. (Pro tip: maybe both of you should be in on the joke, or feelings could get messy.)

This law leads to some comically absurd possibilities. Imagine a reality show where contestants dare each other into quickie weddings, then race to Delaware to annul. It's marriage as a competitive sport – and Delaware as the referee blowing the whistle, "Foul! No real intent. Points off, marriage nullified!" It also casts an interesting light on impulsive unions in general. Vegas weddings are notorious for this sort of thing (Britney Spears' 55-hour marriage, anyone?). Most places, those couples have to plead intoxication or fraud or some vague reason to undo the oopsie. But Delaware straight-up acknowledges human folly. It's like the state looked at the institution of marriage – supposedly sacred and serious – and then looked at us clowns and said, *"We know y'all sometimes treat this like a game of truth-or-dare. We'll be here to tidy up after you."*

Culturally, it's a wink and a nod to the fact that sometimes people just do stupid things for laughs. It's almost refreshing that the law isn't being a dour parent wagging its finger. Instead, it's saying, *"We get it. Mistakes (and dares) happen. We'll fix it, no lasting harm done."* Of course, it also subtly screams: maybe don't make lifelong promises as a joke? But hey, peer pressure and tequila are a powerful combo. One minute you're shouting "YOLO!" and marrying your spring break fling; the next minute you're praying for a legal reset.

Marriage lesson: The Delaware dare rule shows the law rolling its eyes and sighing, *"OK, fine, we'll clean up your mess."* It's society admitting that while marriage is serious, people aren't always. We're impulsive, we're silly, and sometimes we play chicken with major life decisions. The fact this law exists is both funny and telling: it acknowledges a contradiction in how we view marriage. On one hand, *"'Til death do us part"* – on the other, *"Haha, just kidding!"* Delaware basically codified a mulligan for matrimony. The lesson here? Maybe don't treat marriage like a dare in the first place. But if you do, it's nice to know the law has a heart (and a sense of humor) about it. It's a reminder that even our legal system knows humans are imperfect – and occasionally downright ridiculous – in love.

Proxy Knots and Telephone "I Dos"

They say love knows no distance – and boy, do some marriage laws take that literally. Why settle for being in the same room (or planet) as your spouse when you say your vows? Welcome to the wild world of proxy marriages, where "stand-ins" and phone lines can seal the deal.

If you thought planning a wedding was hard when your partner is across the country, try when they're in outer space. Yes, that happened too – we'll get there. But first stop: Montana, USA, the holy grail for couples who can't physically attend their own wedding. In Big Sky Country, you can be married by proxy – meaning someone else stands at the altar for you – and Montana is the only state that even allows a double proxy marriage where *neither* of you shows up. It's like sending stunt doubles to do your wedding scene because the stars are busy filming on location. Quite literally, you can be chillin' in two different places (or war zones) while designated hitters exchange your rings.

Why on earth (or off earth) would this be a thing? The answer, as with many strange laws, lies in necessity and a touch of romance. Montana's proxy marriage law originated to help military couples. Picture a young soldier in Afghanistan who can't get leave, and his sweetheart back home in Kentucky who doesn't want to wait another year to tie the knot. Montana says, *"No problem, we got this."* As long as one of them is a Montana resident or in the military, two proxies (basically, willing volunteers or appointed folks) can stand in for the bride and groom and go through the motions. They sign the papers, say the "I do" on behalf of the couple, and presto – the far-flung lovers are legally married without ever being in the same time zone. It's equal parts heartwarming and surreal. Imagine explaining to your grandkids that grandma and grandpa *technically* weren't at their own wedding – but don't worry, some strangers in Montana did a fine job filling in.

This practice isn't entirely new – during World Wars, proxy marriages happened when soldiers couldn't return home. Some ceremonies were done via telephone lines crackling with static as vows were spoken an ocean apart. So Montana's law is like a quaint holdover that found new life. By the 2000s, it became more than a wartime thing; it turned into a mini industry. Lawyers and officiants in Montana started offering "double proxy wedding" services. For a fee, they'll handle all the paperwork, hire two stand-ins to sign on the dotted line for bride and groom, and file the marriage certificate. The couple gets a nice legal document proving they're hitched – even if their first kiss as spouses has to wait until they're in the same ZIP code again. It's the Amazon Prime of weddings: you could essentially get married remotely, quick and (relatively) easy. No need to elope to Vegas; just send your love to Montana's courthouse by FedEx.

Now, about that outer space wedding. In 2003, a Texas bride named Ekaterina was on Earth, and her groom – Russian cosmonaut Yuri Malenchenko – was literally orbiting above in the International Space Station. They didn't want to postpone the marriage (cosmic love waits for no one), so they used a proxy system. Yuri gave power of attorney to a stand-in on Earth. During the ceremony, Ekaterina stood in a wedding gown in Houston, and a buddy of Yuri's stood in for him because, well, groom was busy doing science in zero gravity. They even had a phone hookup so Yuri could say "I do" from space – presumably floating with a view of Earth out the window. This was arguably the first space marriage. NASA was reportedly not too keen on the idea initially (there were concerns like, "Is this legal? What if the Russians beam *Here Comes the Bride* through our comms?"). But in the end, love triumphed over bureaucratic hesitation. They signed the papers proxy-style and made galactic history. If that isn't an argument that distance is just a number, I don't know what is. Long-distance relationship? Try 220 miles above the earth moving at 17,000 mph. Beat that, Zoom couples.

Speaking of Zoom, let's talk pandemic weddings. When COVID-19 hit, suddenly *everyone* was doing a long-distance marriage of sorts. In 2020, with lockdowns in place, many jurisdictions (New York, for example) temporarily legalized virtual weddings. Couples got married over video calls – a officiant on one screen, the pair on another, family members watching muted (and probably in pajamas) from wherever. What was once a Montana oddity became a global necessity. We saw drive-by weddings, Facebook Live weddings, even *Animal Crossing* video game weddings (yes, people used a video game to host their ceremonies!). In a weird way, Montana's proxy approach was ahead of its time. Those folks in Helena, MT could smugly say, *"Remote wedding? Been doing that for years, welcome to the club."* Society at large had to embrace the idea that a marriage could be real even if the parties aren't in the same chapel exchanging rings physically.

Of course, not everyone loves the idea of proxy marriages. Some find it too detached, fearing it cheapens the sanctity of the ceremony. There's the joke about someone else saying *"I do"* for you – hope they said it with feeling! And you better really trust your proxy not to get the names wrong or burst out laughing. But for those who use it, it's a lifesaver. Military couples got to access benefits and peace of mind of being officially married even while oceans apart. Immigrants sometimes wed by proxy to start visa processes sooner. And let's be honest, for introverts who hate big weddings, the idea of outsourcing your own wedding might sound secretly appealing: *"Honey, why don't we skip the fuss, hire two people to do it for us, and we'll celebrate later?"* It's almost like hiring wedding planners to the extreme – they even stand in for you.

Marriage lesson: The proxy marriage phenomenon shows that marriage is ultimately about the commitment, not the pageantry. When life throws obstacles – war, distance, pandemics, or low Earth orbit – love finds a way, and the law (at least in some cool places like Montana) says, *"Alright, we'll make it work somehow."* It's a quirky reminder that while we picture weddings as this ultra-personal, in-person experience, what truly matters is the legal and emotional bond. Whether you're hand-in-hand under an altar, or saying vows through a crackly phone line, or signing papers via proxies, the result is the same on paper: you're married. Society's rules around marriage have had to bend to technology, necessity, and, frankly, the absurd lengths people will go to be together. And guess what? The institution of marriage survived just fine. In fact, it got more inclusive of unusual situations. Love laughs at distance, and once in a while, the law chuckles along and says "sure, why not – love is love, even if you have to hire a stand-in to say so." When you see laws adapt like this, you realize marriage isn't about how you celebrate, it's about why – and the why (love, commitment, partnership) can thrive even in the strangest of circumstances.

Weird Wedlock World Tour

Pack your bags and your sense of humor – it's time for a global tour of marital madness. Around the world, cultures have cooked up some truly bizarre marriage laws and customs. These odd rules are like funhouse mirrors reflecting each society's quirks about love, commitment, and breaking up. From banishing divorce parties in the Outback, to requiring a roof for your "I do" in London, to literally fearing that an electric fan could end your honeymoon in Seoul – the world's wedding laws are a trip. Let's journey through a few favorites, and see what they say about how wonderfully weird love can be.

First stop: Australia. Land of kangaroos, Crocodile Dundee, and… no divorce parties? That's right – apparently Aussies don't want you turning a divorce into a rager. Culturally and legally, there's an understanding Down Under that divorce is a solemn thing, not an excuse to pop champagne and hire a DJ. In fact, Australia's family law system requires couples to be separated for one whole year before a divorce is granted. That built-in pause button is kind of the opposite of impulsive Vegas weddings – it's like, *"Oi, take a breath, mates. Think it over."* And while it's not like police will bust down your door if you celebrate finally signing the papers, throwing an extravagant divorce party is seen as poor form. There have even been social media dust-ups over people posting cheeky "Just Divorced!" selfies or hosting big bashes to toast the end of their marriage – met with public tut-tutting. Essentially, Australia bans the party in "parting." The idea is divorce isn't something to cheer on like a football match; it's more of a last resort to be handled with a bit of dignity (and maybe a quiet beer with a friend, *not* a wild night at the pub with "Single Ladies" blaring). So if you're in Oz and your divorce gets finalized, maybe keep the streamers and cake low-key. The law won't jail you for that "Freedom at last!" keg stand, but society's judgment might. The Aussie lesson: even in splitsville, keep it classy – no victory laps for failed marriages.

Next: England. Ah, the English – known for tradition, propriety, and apparently a deep suspicion of the outdoors. For centuries, English law had what we'll call the "roof requirement." Basically, you couldn't legally get married outside under open sky. No beach weddings, no garden arbors, no saying vows under a romantic oak tree – not unless you fancied your marriage invalid. The law insisted the ceremony take place in a fixed structure with a roof (church, registry office, or later on, a licensed venue). Rain or shine, that union better have a ceiling above it! Legend has it this odd rule dates back to the Marriage Act of 1836 and other Victorian-era regulations aiming to standardize weddings and keep them from turning into free-for-all elopements in fields. The Brits love order, and what's more orderly than four walls and a roof, right? This led to some amusing workaround scenes: Couples who dreamed of an outdoor wedding would do the official bit indoors (even if just under a gazebo or in a doorway to satisfy the law) and then move the party outside. Imagine a sunny English garden, all decorated for a wedding – but the bride and groom and officiant are huddled under a little porch because legally that's the only spot that counts. It sounds like a Monty Python sketch, but it was reality. Only in recent years did England finally relax this rule. As of 2021, outdoor civil weddings became possible (cheers to modernity!). Still, for a very long time, the British attitude was "you may kiss the bride – but do it *indoors*, you hooligans." It speaks to a charming, if a bit stodgy, notion that marriage needed literally to have a solid roof over it, perhaps symbolizing the shelter and structure of society overseeing your union. Or maybe they just didn't trust the famously fickle British weather and figured weddings are chaotic enough without wind and rain mucking it up. Lesson from London: Tradition dies hard. Sometimes laws stick around well past their sell-by date, requiring a dash of common sense (and reform) to catch up with what couples actually want. In love, as in real estate, it used to be all about "location, location, location" – and in old England, that location had to have a roof.

Onward to South Korea. This one's less about marriage ceremonies and more about surviving to enjoy married life. South Korea has a well-known *superstition* that took on an almost legal-life of its own: electric fan death. The belief is that if you fall asleep in a closed room with a fan running, you might never wake up. According to the legend, the fan could cause hypothermia or suck out the oxygen – basically, the fan becomes an uninvited *Grim Reaper*. Now, this isn't officially written in the marriage code or anything, but it's so prevalent that it influenced consumer safety regulations. To this day, fans sold in Korea often come with timers and warning labels by strong recommendation, effectively making it a de facto law of the land that fans shouldn't run all night. Government agencies have put out summer safety bulletins about it, and headlines will attribute certain unfortunate deaths to "fan death." It's wild – doctors globally roll their eyes, but many Koreans, especially older folks, swear by it. So how does this connect to marriage? Well, imagine it's your wedding night in Seoul, middle of a steamy summer. You and your spouse are in a tiny apartment with no AC. You innocently go to flick on the oscillating fan for some breeze. Cue your Korean mother-in-law shrieking, *"Noooo! Not while you sleep!"* She might insist you use the timer so it shuts off after 30 minutes – for your own safety. Romantic, huh? Nothing sets the mood like, *"Sweet dreams dear, I set the fan to turn off so it doesn't murder us in our sleep. Kisses!"* It's an example of how even a quirk like a superstition can embed itself so deeply in a culture that the laws and products adapt to it. Sure, it's not explicitly a marriage law, but any foreign spouse moving to Korea quickly learns this "rule" of domestic life. Defying it might not get you arrested, but you'll get such side-eye from the locals (and especially the in-laws) that you might wish it were just a fine. Lesson: Love and marriage often come bundled with cultural quirks your partner grew up with – some of which can be downright bizarre. You can laugh, but you also respect it (or at least set that fan timer to keep the peace). In a broader sense, this shows how laws or guidelines sometimes arise from folklore or fears rather than scientific fact – a contradiction between what's *true* and what people *feel*. And in relationships, as in law, feelings often win.

Now for some kissing bans – because what tour of weird love laws would be complete without telling people where, when, and whom they can smooch? Let's start in the romance capital, France. Believe it or not, France has (or had) a law banning kissing on train platforms. Oui, *c'est vrai!* Since 1910, it was technically illegal for lovestruck couples to engage in prolonged farewells at the train station. The reasoning? These amorous goodbyes were apparently causing delays – trains can't leave on time if Pierre and Juliette are locked in a dramatic embrace blocking the door. So the authorities said, enough, save it for later – or at least take it off the platform. Was it ever enforced? Hard to say. It's hard to imagine gendarmes prying apart entwined lovers yelling "Arrêtez! Pas de baiser ici!" But the fact that it was on the books tells you how even the French, infamous for public displays of affection, have their limits when public transit efficiency is at stake. It's delightfully ironic: the country that coined "French kiss" has a law saying "please don't, at least not right before the 8:05 to Lyon." Meanwhile, across the Channel, the Brits had (and maybe still have on the books) some truly goofy snogging statutes. One oft-cited old law in England supposedly forbade kissing on Sundays in public. Puritans really said "Keep holy the Sabbath – and keep your lips to yourselves." Over in the United States, a patchwork of antiquated local laws will give you a chuckle: In Connecticut, it was illegal for a man to kiss his wife on a Sunday in public (apparently God wasn't the only one resting that day). In Colorado's Logan County, there was a law that a man cannot kiss a sleeping woman (we'll charitably interpret that as a consent issue – Snow White and Sleeping Beauty would be lawbreakers there). Perhaps the silliest – and most meme-able – are those "mustache laws." It's often claimed that in some American towns back in the day, if you had a mustache, you were forbidden from kissing women. The idea being maybe whisker burns were a scourge on female cheeks? Whether those were real laws or just apocryphal, they've stuck in the public imagination. We can't help picturing a Victorian-era sheriff wagging a finger at a handlebar-mustached gent: *"Remove those lips from that lady, sir, or shave that atrocity at once!"* All these kissing bans, in sum, reveal a historical obsession with policing intimacy, either for moral reasons or, hilariously, for logistical ones (looking at you, French trains). Lesson: Love may be universal, but kissing apparently needed a rulebook. These odd restrictions highlight the tension between private affection and public decorum. Society oscillates between *"Get a room!"* and *"Aww, how sweet."* The fact that many of these laws are defunct or ignored now shows that love (and common sense) eventually win out. People are gonna kiss – no matter what some 1910 railway statute says. Good luck enforcing the unspoken rule that newlyweds *will* smooch for their photos, even if a sign says "No kissing." When law and love collide, love usually finds a loophole.

Finally, a grab-bag of other odd wedlock statutes from our journey: In Wichita, Kansas, it's reportedly grounds for divorce if a man mistreats his mother-in-law. That's right – if you can't play nice with her mom, you might be legally shown the door. Is this a law or just a genius idea? (Some moms-in-law no doubt approved that legislation with a wink.) Over in Truro, Massachusetts circa 1770s, a local law demanded that any bachelor wanting to marry had to kill a certain number of blackbirds or crows first – a bizarre marriage dowry via pest control. We assume that one's off the books now, but it's a window into how marriage used to be tangled up with community duties ("Prove you can provide... by providing dead birds, apparently.") In Vermont, an old law required a woman to get her husband's permission to wear false teeth. Nothing says true love like "Honey, may I have your blessing to get dentures?" That law screams 19th century gender roles (and dental tech) at its finest – and reminds us how far we've come. And in Kentucky, there's a legendary law that a woman can't marry the *same* man more than three times. Marry, divorce, remarry, repeat... but after round three, the Commonwealth of Kentucky taps you on the shoulder like a sensible friend and says, *"Darlin', no. This merry-go-round stops now."* You gotta appreciate that one – it's as if the law is preventing the ultimate on-again, off-again toxic relationship cycle. If you haven't figured it out by the third divorce, you two are *done*, says Kentucky. In the global context, there are places where the absence of a law is the weird part – for example, the Philippines has no divorce at all (except for special cases or religions). If you marry in Manila, you better be sure, because legally it's one-and-done (unless you navigate the thorny annulment process or move to another country). It's almost the polar opposite of Delaware's easy annulments: the Philippines basically says "No exit, try counseling." Meanwhile, Saudi Arabia only recently let women drive and still has some strict guardianship rules affecting marriage, and India in 2019 banned an instant divorce practice (the "triple talaq" in Muslim communities) to protect women from capricious repudiation. These aren't funny like mustache laws, but they show oddities in how different places handle who can leave whom and how.

Having toured the world's strangest marriage laws, one thing stands out: love makes people crazy, and people make laws to try to civilize the crazy. Sometimes the laws are just as loopy as the love stories. They range from sweetly bizarre (marrying a dead fiancé out of devotion) to sternly bizarre (no party when you divorce, you heathens). They can be born from tragedy, practicality, superstition, or plain old nosy moralizing. What they all have in common is they reflect the values, fears, and eccentricities of the society that created them. It's like each law carries a little story about the culture: the French value romantic fidelity so deeply they'll marry the dead; Delaware knows humans are goofballs; the English treasured order and formality in marriage to an almost comedic degree; Koreans would rather be safe (or superstitious) than sorry in the bedroom; and many an American town council once thought they should be the kiss police.

Marriage lesson: Laws about love can be just as kooky as love itself. When you line them all up, you realize that marriage – ostensibly a universal institution – is reinvented in a thousand ways by different cultures. It's society's attempt to put boundaries and frameworks around that wild little thing called love. And often, it succeeds only in highlighting our contradictions. We say marriage is sacred and serious... then we make laws about dares and ghost weddings and mother-in-laws and mustaches that sound straight out of a sitcom. It's hilariously human. In the end, these oddball laws serve as a mirror, showing us that for all our pomp and ceremony, we're an inventive, emotional, and sometimes absurd bunch when it comes to matrimony. Love can inspire us to bend rules, break rules, or write completely new ones. And while the rules may try to tame love's chaos, they often just document it. The big takeaway? Don't take it all too seriously. Marriage is a social construct, sure, but it's built by *people* – fallible, passionate, weird people. The laws will change, the customs will evolve, but the fundamental quirkiness of human love remains. So here's to the legal laughs and lessons Cupid leaves in his wake – may they remind us that when it comes to love and law, sometimes truth really is stranger (and funnier) than fiction.

Epilogue

For those who think love is merely a private affair with no real-world repercussions, the tales in this book beg to differ. Time and again, love has proven itself a cheeky, transformative force — one that doesn't just break rules, but writes new ones. As we've seen, Cupid's arrows can topple church doors, court rulings, and even royal crowns, all while wearing a mischievous grin.

Consider the historical heavyweights: King Henry VIII was so smitten (or at least desperate for an heir) that he severed England from the Catholic Church just to ditch his wife and marry Anne Boleyn. Centuries later, his great-great-nephew Edward VIII literally gave up the British throne to marry Wallis Simpson, proving that even kings will chuck it all for love. And far from palaces, in 1856 India, an 11-year-old widow named Kalimati Devi made history when her remarriage – the first legal widow remarriage – boldly defied centuries of tradition. Talk about love upending the establishment.

Love also thumbed its nose at discriminatory norms. Frederick Douglass quietly wed Helen Pitts, a white woman, in 1884, prompting gasps and a classic Douglass quip that his first wife was the color of his mother and his second the color of his father. In 1967, Mildred and Richard Loving (with a last name fit for the storybooks) got the U.S. Supreme Court to strike down interracial marriage bans. And long before same-sex marriage was law, Jack Baker and Michael McConnell in Minnesota obtained a marriage license in 1971 – decades ahead of the curve and unafraid to make history in the name of love.

So, what's the takeaway from these unruly romances? Simply that love, in all its witty and rebellious glory, is a catalyst for progress. When hearts defiantly unite, they nudge society forward – sometimes with a courtroom victory, sometimes with a royal resignation, always with a wink. The lovers in these pages show that however strict the rule or high the wall, love will find a way to leap over and leave the world a little more open in its wake. In short, love always wins – often in the most unexpected and rebellious ways. Whether bridging age gaps, breaking racial barriers, or rewriting laws, love finds a way – and the rest of us are better off for the ride.

www.ingramcontent.com/pod-product-compliance
Lightning Source LLC
Chambersburg PA
CBHW061805120626
46550CB00005B/2142